Stanley Milgram

Other titles in Mind Shapers Series

*Sigmund Freud* by Richard Stevens

*Erik Erikson* by Richard Stevens

*George Kelly* by Trevor Butt

*Burrhus F. Skinner* by Frederick Toates

*Erich Fromm* by Annette Thompson

# milgram
### Stanley

## understanding obedience
## and its implications

**Peter Lunt**

*Professor of Media and Communications, Brunel University of West London*

Mind Shapers – Key Psychologists and their impact
Series Editor: Richard Stevens

## palgrave
## macmillan

First published in paperback 2009 by
PALGRAVE MACMILLAN

Palgrave Macmillan in the UK is an imprint of Macmillan Publishers Limited, registered in England, company number 785998, of Houndmills, Basingstoke, Hampshire RG21 6XS.

Palgrave Macmillan in the US is a division of St Martin's Press LLC, 175 Fifth Avenue, New York, NY 10010.

Palgrave Macmillan is the global academic imprint of the above companies and has companies and representatives throughout the world.

Palgrave® and Macmillan® are registered trademarks in the United States, the United Kingdom, Europe and other countries

ISBN-13: 978–0–230–57315–4

This book is printed on paper suitable for recycling and made from fully managed and sustained forest sources. Logging, pulping and manufacturing processes are expected to conform to the environmental regulations of the country of origin.

A catalogue record for this book is available from the British Library.

A catalog record for this book is available from the Library of Congress.

10  9  8  7  6  5  4  3  2  1
18  17  16  15  14  13  12  11  10  09

Printed and bound in Great Britain by
CPI Antony Rowe, Chippenham and Eastbourne

# Contents

# Acknowledgements

First, I would like to thank the teachers who inspired my interest in social psychology: Peter Kelvin and Adrian Furnham were both brilliant teachers at undergraduate level. During my PhD Jos Jaspers, Mansur Lalljee and Michael Argyle established a context for discussion of ideas and research in social psychology that I have never seen equalled. There are individuals who I have talked to or written to as I have been writing this book and who, sometimes through a simple suggestion have had an influence that has helped me enormously: Richard Butsch, Daniel Dayan, Rodney Livingstone, Elihu Katz, Sonia Livingstone, Amit Pinchevski, Chris Rojek, Paul Stenner, Ziyad Marar, Bruce Williams, Mila Steele, Anna Livingstone and Joe Livingstone come most to mind. Richard Stevens provided sage advice and excellent feedback on the draft manuscript and Todd Motto helped me by editing the book. I would also like to thank the many students over 16 years who took my lectures on Milgram in the UCL psychology department; it was fun and it has been a pleasure to write what I had only spoken for so many years.

There are always key texts that have a defining influence when one is researching a book. First and foremost the writings of Milgram himself, Thomas Blass's biography of Milgram is excellent, Arthur Miller's book on the reaction of the psychological community to Milgram's research, Zygmunt Bauman on the Holocaust, Todd Gitlin and John Lewis Gladdis on post-war US history, David Held on critical theory and models of democracy, Evans on The Third Reich, Katherine Pandora's brilliant book on the liberal, pragmatist tradition in social psychology, and Jonathan Joseph on conflict, cohesion and consent in social theory.

To Sonia, Joe and Anna

# Preface

What would you do if a professor asked you to administer painful electric shocks to someone as part of a psychology experiment? Is unethical research practice justified if it is driven by a higher moral purpose? Would you stand up to an authority figure if you believed they were in the wrong? Does power in modern societies rely on public apathy and passivity? How much does democracy depend upon the ability of individuals to bring those in power to account? In the work of Stanley Milgram, these questions were brought down from the ivory tower and examined in his psychology research lab.

In 1963, Stanley Milgram, a young psychology professor at Yale University published a paper in which he described an experimental study of obedience to authority. There are thousands of academic papers written in psychology every year but this one was different; the design of the experiment was controversial and the results were extraordinary and disconcerting. Milgram reported the results from a procedure in which ordinary American citizens from the New Haven area of Connecticut volunteered to play the teacher in a role-play experiment concerning the potential value of punishment for learning. In what appeared to be a simple memory task, the experimenter instructed the participants as 'teachers' to give electric shocks to another person playing the role of the learner every time the learner made a mistake. At first, the shocks were mild, but the experimenter instructed the teacher to raise the shock level each time the learner made a mistake. As the level of the shocks rose to around 100 volts, the person receiving them screamed with pain and pleaded to be released from the experiment. Although some of the volunteers objected to giving the shocks at this point, alarmingly 65% of them carried on obeying the commands of the experimenter even when the shocks reached lethal levels and the person receiving the shocks was silent, apparently unconscious or dead. How was it possible that people were so obedient to the authority of the experimenter that they were prepared to inflict serious harm, even death, on fellow human beings? Why did they not protest and refuse to follow the orders of the experimenter?

The experiments captured the public imagination and Milgram become a minor celebrity (a very early example of the celebrity academic). People are rightly both fascinated and appalled by the results of his study because they challenge their beliefs about how they would behave when asked by an authority to harm another person. We assume we would surely act on our conscience and disobey the experimenter, but the experiments make us doubt this and bring into question our view of ourselves as moral and independent individuals. In addition, the experiments have implications for a variety of social, political and moral questions of great importance. For example, at the time that Milgram was conducting his experiments in the USA, Adolf Eichmann, an administrator in Nazi Germany who had played a role in the organisation of genocide during World War II was on trial in Israel. The Eichmann trial attracted worldwide media attention and revealed accounts of the events of the Holocaust and the mechanisms of horror in the Nazi regime. Hannah Arendt, a critical social philosopher who attended the early part of the trial was struck by the idea that Eichmann came across as a typical bureaucrat who otherwise led an ordinary life, not as a psychopath, ideologue or evil monster; he appeared to demonstrate the banality of evil. This interpretation of Eichmann as an ordinary person swept up in evil events reflects the conclusion that Milgram drew from his obedience experiments that evil deeds are not necessarily perpetrated by evil people. The results appeared to demonstrate that evil was not the result of a lingering primitiveness in society or the release of primeval destructive emotions but arose from the normal practices of modern society. The modern world, populated by people who are arguably freer than at any time at history, might yet turn out to be the most destructive age because individuals are ineffective in the face of the highly organised forms of power that characterise their society.

Milgram's experiment also raises important questions about the operation of power and the political culture of post-war USA and more general questions about the levels of moral autonomy and political engagement of citizens in liberal democracy. What is extraordinary about Milgram's creative intelligence is that he was able to take these questions of political autonomy – the impact of authority and social pressure on individuals, the ethics of personal responsibility and political subjectivity – and express these complex, interconnected themes in a single, powerful role-play experiment. The performance of the participants in the experiments, their vulnerability and their humanity, the elegance of the design all come together to demand our attention and concern. Consequently, this book starts with the experiments, which are the basis for Milgram's fame and his greatest achievement and outlines the design and results of the experiments and the variations that Milgram conducted. Although the results of the experiments were extraordinary and had a major impact in academic psychology, in other academic disciplines, and amongst the public, they were roundly criticised by his peers. Therefore, I devote a chapter to these criticisms, which raise important questions about the ethics of experimental work in social psychology and a range of detailed but fascinating methodological challenges and reflections on what science can offer to our understanding of human beings as social animals.

This book also examines the broader impact of Milgram's era on his work; post-war USA claimed to be the freest society on earth and yet it was bedevilled by paradoxes and contradictions. There was growing and widespread affluence, which gave new freedoms for citizens of the new consumer society, and yet there was a feeling that society was fragmented and alienating. Although the USA was a liberal democracy, there was a great deal of apathy and conformity; people seemed to lack engagement and commitment to public life. The USA was the most powerful economy and military regime in the world, yet there were widespread insecurities arising from the Cold War, the development of the bomb and social shifts that were changing people's lives.

Milgram's research and writings reflect these paradoxes; his participants appeared to demonstrate the vulnerability of ordinary Americans, their lack of moral fibre and the dangers of social control and manipulation. Milgram's experiment captured the feeling of his day: critical concerns about the isolation, alienation and vulnerability of American citizens. Milgram grew up in this *Zeitgeist*. The threat of nuclear destruction, the covert operations of the CIA and the threat of competition from state socialism created an atmosphere of fear and a culture of conformity.

I will argue that Milgram's approach, which took questions and ideas from social and political theory, from history, from moral philosophy and from psychology and explored them through examining the behaviour and reactions of individuals in the psychology lab, represents experimental social psychology at its best. Throughout the book, I aim to demonstrate the relevance of social psychological research and theory to key social, political and moral questions that go to the heart of what it means to be an individual in a liberal democracy.

Although the book focuses on the history of Milgram's ideas, the character of Milgram himself runs through the book like a vibrant thread, just as his character shone in his lifetime. I am indebted to Blass's biography of Stanley Milgram *The Man Who Shocked the World*, which I have read with great pleasure. His sympathetic but critical account of Milgram the man and his works provided a foundation upon which I have explored the broader intellectual climate, content and reception of Milgram's ideas.

# 1 Milgram's Obedience to Authority Experiments

## An invitation

Imagine you are reading your local paper one day and a public announcement catches your eye calling for volunteers to take part in a study of memory at your local university and promising to pay you a small amount of money plus expenses for your time. The announcement goes on to say that no special qualifications are needed to take part and lists a range of jobs illustrating that a variety of people are being sought. At the bottom of the announcement there is a form for potential volunteers to fill in. You are intrigued and decide to fill in the form giving your name, address, telephone number, age, occupation and sex, whether you can participate on weekdays, evenings or weekends and the best time to call you. A little while later you receive a phone call from the university asking you to arrange a time to participate in the study, you agree on a time and are told the location. On the appointed day you travel to the university campus, you are slightly nervous as you have never been there before but you follow the signs to a modern building, locate the room and enter to find two men waiting for you. One, a professional looking man in his 30s wearing a grey scientists lab coat says 'hello', explains that he is the experimenter and introduces you to another, mild looking, middle aged man who, like you, is a volunteer in the study.

The scientist then explains that the study you have agreed to participate in aims to find out if punishment can improve performance on a simple memory test. You and the other volunteer draw lots to see who will play the role of the teacher in the study and who will play the role of the learner. The experimenter invites you and your fellow participant to draw lots; you both draw slips of paper. One of the slips of paper has the word 'learner' and the other 'teacher' and you draw the one with 'teacher' on it. You then accompany the experimenter and the 'learner' to the room

1

next-door and watch the learner being seated in a chair, strapped in and having an electrode fixed to his wrist by the experimenter. You return to the other room and the experimenter instructs you to sit in front of a large piece of electrical equipment that has a series of switches. The switches are labelled with voltage levels starting at 15 and going up in 15-volt intervals to a maximum of 450 volts. You receive a mild electric shock to demonstrate what the learner will experience during the experiment.

At last, the study starts and you ask the first question. You read out a pair of words (e.g. blue box, nice day, wild duck) and then ask the 'learner' to name the word paired with one that you read out. If they get the answer right then you go on to the next question. However, if they give the wrong answer then you press a button to administer an electric shock (15 volts the first time, then 30 volts, then 45 volts and so on adding 15 volts each time there is a wrong answer).

At first things seem okay; you ask the questions, administer the shocks when a wrong answer is given and, following the experimenter's prompts, you raise the voltage level. The learner does not respond when you give them the initial shocks. However, as the voltage level rises to 100 volts you hear his first reactions to the shocks. You feel apprehensive as the learner calls out in pain and you look across at the experimenter who seems to be calm so you carry on. The shock levels get even higher, the learner starts to protest, shouting, screaming with pain and demanding to be released. You feel very uncomfortable and upset at this point and you turn to the experimenter suggesting that something is going wrong with the experiment and that you are concerned about the learner. The experimenter responds in a matter of fact voice asking you to continue. You carry on but the screams are getting louder and the learner complains that they have a heart condition so you turn again to the experimenter and receive another bland reply telling you to continue with the experiment. Again, despite your misgivings, despite the screams of the learner, despite feeling a combination of anger and distress you carry on asking the questions and administrating the shocks.

At about 300 volts, something extraordinary happens; the learner stops responding. You are worried that he might have fainted or even died and you turn to the experimenter who again tells you to continue with the experiment. You ask how you can since the person is no longer answering your questions, but the experimenter tells you to treat no answer as a wrong answer so you press the switch to administer a 315 volt shock and raise the level to 330. By now you have asked many questions and administered 22 shocks, you just want this to end and continue to 450 volts by which time you have delivered 30 shocks to the learner and nine or ten since you felt that he had either fainted, had a heart attack or died.

The experimenter says that you have completed the experiment and explains the background of the study to you. With astonishment, you hear that the learner had been pretending and did not in fact receive any shocks. What you had been hearing were not his screams of agony resulting from electric shocks that you were delivering but a tape that he had recorded earlier in which he acted out reactions to different levels of shock. The experimenter introduces the learner to you and he confirms that he was play-acting all the time and never received a single shock! This has been an upsetting, difficult, highly uncomfortable experience. You listen in surprise as the experimenter tells you that you have not been participating in a study of memory but a study of the psychology of obedience to authority aiming to find out the conditions under which individuals are prepared to harm others when they are ordered to do so. You try to explain to the experimenter how you had felt during the experiment and to give an explanation for why you went along with the deception and, although it was a role-play, the reasons why you carried on despite your evident unhappiness.

Later you hear about the experiments, which have become quite a talking point, and the person responsible for them, a social psychologist called Stanley Milgram has become quite a public figure, appearing in documentaries and in magazine articles. You have been a subject in one of the most famous experiments in psychology (perhaps second only to Pavlov's dogs): Stanley Milgram's experiments on obedience to authority.

## Stanley Milgram

Despite his early death of heart failure at the age of 51, Stanley Milgram had a long and distinguished career as an academic social psychologist. I will discuss a number of examples of his empirical work and writings in this book. However, what made Milgram famous was the series of experiments on obedience to authority that he conducted very early in his career when he was a young assistant professor at Yale and just after the completion of his PhD.

Although the series of experiments that Milgram conducted between 1960 and 1963 were to gain immediate recognition, even fame, he did not write up the full account of the obedience experiments until his 1974 book *Obedience to Authority*. Milgram published a small number of the studies in the academic literature along with more popular articles describing the experiments, which turned out to be important for the reception of Milgram's work. The study reported in his first paper published in 1963 was Milgram's baseline study in which he set out to establish a procedure that would put participants in a conflict situation that was meaningful to them and through which he could generate a simple measure of the level of obedience. Milgram's intention was to use this 'procedure' or baseline condition in what he saw as the real business of his experiments: to manipulate the conditions under which people received orders from authority to see which situational factors influence the level of obedience. Milgram drew a distinction between his 'procedure' and his subsequent experiments and as a scientist, he was careful to claim that causal accounts could only be given when he designed manipulations of the conditions under which people were exposed to commands from an authority figure. Many of the manipulations that Milgram subsequently introduced reduced the level of obedience, so the notoriety that Milgram's study achieved is exacerbated because the initial procedure produced amongst the highest levels of obedience and 'harm' to the learner.

Yet it was the first study, the demonstration of obedience, which caught the academic and public imagination because the results of the study were both unexpected and alarming. Sixty five percent of the participants in the study described above completed the experiment and administered 450 volts to an apparently unconscious or dead learner. Apparently normal citizens of the USA in the early 1960s agreed to inflict serious harm on people who they thought were fellow volunteers when asked to do so by a scientific investigator. The findings are sensational and evocative and leave us with as many questions as answers. The experimental context resonates with the Holocaust, bringing to mind the excesses of the Nazi regime and the genocide committed during the Second World War. Worse still, the experiment took place in the USA in the early 1960s in an apparently free liberal democracy not against the backdrop of a totalitarian regime. Furthermore, the experimenter had no real power over the participants who as volunteers could, in principle, have walked out of the experiment at any point. These points raise uncomfortable questions about the nature of genocide and the assumption that evil deeds arise from evil minds. The participants in Milgram's studies were ordinary American citizens, not homicidal maniacs, psychopaths or evil people. They left the experiment and returned to their families and workplaces to lead normal, respectable lives.

Milgram tapped into the ideas that the political theorist Hannah Arendt had developed in reaction to the arrest and trial of the Nazi war criminal Adolf Eichmann for whom she coined the phrase 'the banality of evil'. Eichmann was an administrator in Nazi Germany with responsibility for organising part of the logistics that supported the transportation and running of the extermination camps during the Holocaust. However, the man who appeared in the courtroom in Jerusalem in the early 1960s had more in common with a civil servant than the popular image of a mass murderer. Against this background, Milgram's findings suggested that we might all be capable of inflicting harm on others in the right circumstances. Although some of the participants in the experiment protested, many of them carried on obeying the commands of the experimenter even though it caused them distress, suggesting a moral weakness of character amongst ordinary American citizens. People appear to be passive conformists who are unable to assert their rights to challenge authority based on their conscience and personal values. What did this tell us about modern, affluent, liberal societies and what did it tell us about ourselves? In addition, Eichmann's occupation as an administrator suggested another frightening idea: that the efficiency of modern societies could, under certain circumstances, lead to terrible social and human consequences rather than to the good life we might hope to live.

In addition to all of these connotations of Milgram's findings, which raise a variety of disturbing social, moral and political questions, the fact that they are so unexpected adds to their fascination. Milgram himself had thought that it would be hard to get people to obey the experimenter in his experiment. When he asked people to predict the results based on a description of the experiment most people predicted far lower levels of obedience than those found in practice. The results are counterintuitive, which makes them good social science because they challenge our assumptions and stereotypes. However, it also suggests that we are carrying around with us, all of us, assumptions about our moral autonomy and independence that may be false. We cherish our sense of ourselves as moral, independent and free and Milgram's experiments bring this into doubt.

Additionally, in liberal democratic society the ability of citizens to challenge authority is, we fondly imagine, critical to what keeps power in check. If individuals are passive in the face of authority what is the value of political freedom and accountability?

These reactions demonstrate the elegance and power of Milgram's experiments on obedience to authority: they are rich with serious implications that raise important questions about the nature of modern society, the operation of power, the role and responsibilities of individuals and their moral character. In this book, I will discuss all these questions but first, in the remainder of this chapter, I will give a more detailed account of the experiments that Milgram completed as reported in his 1974 book *Obedience to Authority*.

## The obedience experiments

Having established that he could induce obedience to authority in an experiment, Milgram set about manipulating the conditions of the experiment to see which variables would influence the level of obedience. Some of the manipulations that Milgram carried out were to check that the experiment was working in the way that he wanted, for example that the context was meaningful to participants. He designed other conditions to rule out alternative explanations for obedience such as the idea that people were expressing latent aggression. The most important manipulations, however, are those in which Milgram tests which social conditions influence the level of obedience, for example, the distance between the participant, the learner and the experimenter.

### Proximity

In Milgram's original procedure, the actor playing the role of the learner was in a separate room from the participant playing the role of the teacher and the experimenter who heard the moans, complaints and screams of the learner through a loudspeaker. In the first condition of his experiments manipulating the proximity of the teacher and the learner, Milgram switched off the loudspeaker so that the teacher could not see the learner, nor could he hear the learner's comments, protests and screams. In this condition, 26 out of 40 people completed the experiment, a lower percentage than the original procedure. In the second condition, the experimenter switched on the loud speaker and otherwise the procedure was the same as the first condition. In this situation, 25 out of 40 participants went to the end of the study. In a third condition, the learner was in the same room as the experimenter and the teacher and obedience reduced to 16 of the 40 participants. In the fourth condition, the learner and teacher sat next to each other and the teacher administered the shocks by pushing the hand of the learner onto an electric plate. In this condition, only 12 out of the 40 participants completed the study. These results demonstrate that the level of obedience to authority increases as the social distance between the learner and the teacher increases.

Milgram discusses a number of possible explanations as to why distance might influence the level of obedience. One possibility is that the visibility of the suffering of another human being provides a powerful cue that increases the empathy the teacher feels for the learner. The Milgram experiment puts the participant playing the role of the teacher in a conflict between obeying authority and following his or her conscience. Empathy makes the identity of the learner salient and might therefore have increased disobedience to the commands of the experimenter. Milgram considers that in the remote conditions it is easier for the teacher to deny the effects that the shocks have on the learner whereas it is more difficult to deny the suffering of the learner when they are in the same room and even more so when they are touching. Milgram suggests that it is more difficult to harm someone who is looking you in the eye and judging your conduct because this makes salient his or her identity as a human being. There are, however, alternative possible explanations as to why obedience levels decline in response to a reduction in the distance between the learner and the teacher. For example, in the remote condition the link between the actions of the teacher and the consequences for the learner are less salient than in the conditions when the effects on the learner are more audible or visible. Alternatively, Milgram suggests that a subtle social psychological effect might result from the fact that the teacher is alone with the experimenter in the remote conditions, which subconsciously draws the teacher into a relationship with the experimenter and 'against' the learner. This interpersonal dynamic changes when the learner is in the same room as the teacher and the experimenter making it less likely that the teacher will take the side of the experimenter.

In his explanations, Milgram draws on a range of social psychological theories. During his PhD studies, he was influenced by the work on conformity by another social psychologist, Solomon Asch. Asch conducted studies of conformity which confronted individuals with a group of people who were all making the same but wrong judgement about the length of lines. In Asch's experiment, people go along with the group decision even if they are clear that the judgement is wrong. However, Asch found that conformity reduced radically when there was more than one independent participant in the group. It appears that the support of a fellow 'real' participant who goes along with their judgements empowers participants to resist the pressure of the majority.

The results of Asch's experiments are open to two different interpretations: that participants respond to the information in the situation that others have made particular judgements or that they simply decide to conform to what the other people are doing in the experiment. In the Milgram experiment, proximity does afford more information, for example, about the effects of the teacher's actions on the learner. Alternatively, participants may be influenced by subtle effects of social conformity, the tendency of individuals to want to get on with other people in a social situation, and they went along with the suggestion of the experimenter. One of the criticisms of Asch's work is that his experiment demonstrates conformity but does not distinguish whether his participants go along with the group norm because they regard this as the best information about the length of the lines or because they want to conform to what other people do. The critical point is that in the different proximity conditions of the Milgram experiment give varying cues to participants about the nature of the task. In the remote conditions, the role of the experimenter is more salient and so people interpret their task as to follow the lead of the experimenter. In contrast, in the proximal conditions, where the teacher is in the same room or touching the learner, they look for clues as to what to do from the learner who is saying that they want to stop the experiment.

The variety of potential explanations also suggests that Milgram did not have a clear rationale for the manipulation of distance in his experiments. Why did Milgram think that social distance would influence the level of obedience? The importance of proximity and the salience of the victim was one of the themes in the very public discussions and debates surrounding Eichmann's arrest and trial and the work of Arendt on the banality of evil. In particular, two important questions emerged in the discussion of the Eichmann trial concerning the organisation of genocide. Did it mean that those who organised it were so distant from its consequences that they experienced no direct moral responsibility? Alternatively, did it mean that there was such strong ideological control over society that individuals felt unable to challenge the orders they were given? Milgram was motivated by his reflections on the Holocaust and the implications that this had for his concerns about the social and political context of his own times. The experiments capture these concerns and raise interesting questions but they do not provide definitive answers. The relationship between Milgram's work, the Holocaust and the political culture of liberal democracy require interpretation. I will return to these questions in more detail in later chapters.

## Variations on the obedience experiments

After this initial round of experiments, Milgram moved his equipment to a more modest urban setting off campus and ran another baseline condition that was similar to the original but introduced the idea that the learner had a heart condition. The results of this baseline condition were similar to the original procedure with 26 out of 40 reaching the end of the experiment, which is almost identical to the 25 in the original study. Milgram also did a study to see if changing the character of the experimenter and the learner would influence the results. In the original experiment, the experimenter was somewhat stiff and formal and the learner was relaxed and friendly. When Milgram reversed these roles so that the learner was formal and the experimenter was friendly there was no significant change in the level of obedience. It appears, therefore, that the personality of the experimenter and the learner had no influence on the level of obedience.

Milgram then ran a number of experiments with his new baseline condition to test new independent variables. For example, developing the theme of distance, Milgram varied the proximity of the experimenter and the teacher and the degree of surveillance employed in the experiments. In one condition, the experimenter sat close to the teacher whereas in another condition, after drawing lots, assigning roles, explaining the procedure and strapping the learner into the chair, the experimenter left the room and gave further instructions over the telephone. When the experimenter was not present, obedience dropped dramatically to nine out of 40. In addition, some participants lied to the experimenter on the phone claiming that they were raising the shock levels but in fact not doing so, indicating that the presence of the experiment binds people to authority in some way. Interestingly, these participants wanted to give the appearance of obedience to the experimenter even when they were disobeying. In one variation, the experimenter would return to the room when disobedience was threatened and under these conditions, obedience went up again.

Up to this point Milgram had only used men in his studies, so he now completed a version of the baseline condition with women and found almost identical levels of obedience, although women reported greater experience of conflict over their role in the experiment during post-experimental interviews. Milgram then conducted a study in response to feedback he had received from debriefing sessions with participants in which they explained that they felt obliged to carry out the orders of the experimenter because they had agreed to take part and had not discussed or negotiated the conditions of the experiment. Milgram introduced a variation in which the learner received the agreement of the experimenter to stop the experiment when he requested it and reminding both the experimenter and the teacher that he has a heart condition. The results showed a drop in obedience to 16 out of 40. Milgram interpreted these results as indicating that the participants were not acting according to an implicit contract, which they believed to exist between themselves and the experimenter. He based this on the finding that this variation in the contract had a small effect on obedience and because disobedient subjects did not mentioned it during debriefing. However, there was a reduction in obedience suggesting that changing the implicit contract between the experimenter and the teacher can affect the degree of obedience.

As a student, Milgram had taken his first degree in political science, switching to social psychology for his graduate studies, and he would have been well aware of the debates over the role that social contracts play in the legitimacy of authority, yet he does not explicitly discuss these ideas in relation to his experimental findings. This is an important aspect of Milgram's work: although he is open to ideas from social or political theory in the development of his research questions and the design of his experiments, he does not interpret his results in relation to these theories but instead offers psychological explanations for obedience to authority. I will take up the theme of the relationship between Milgram's experiments and political theory later in the book.

An issue that participants in earlier experiments had mentioned in post-experiment interviews was that they were obedient because they trusted the university context and the academic researcher. Therefore, Milgram decided to conduct a trial of the baseline condition in a non-university context, reasoning that the association with Yale would give participants a strong sense that they were participating in legitimate and benign research. Milgram set up his equipment and laboratory setting in a nearby industrial town and removed any evidence of a connection to the university in his advertising and instructions. There was a reduction in obedience in the new conditions, suggesting that the authority of the experimenter partly results from the institutional setting of the university, but even so, there was still a high degree of obedience in the experiment conducted in non-university contexts (50% as opposed to 65% in the Yale equivalent). Although Milgram does not explore this idea, his experiment indicates that individuals in modern society place a great deal of trust in institutions.

Giddens (1991) argues that individuals in modern liberal democracies are used to the idea of dealing with the public face of institutions as a relationship of trust. The interaction between the public and representatives of social institutions such as teachers, bosses and public relations specialists shapes the public understanding of social institutions such as universities, firms and government departments. We can presume, therefore, that the participants in the Milgram experiments would have had a high degree of trust in a representative of an academic institution. Participants' deference and their subsequent obedience may have reflected these expectations rather than being the result of a general tendency to obey, which is Milgram's explanation. Participants' disquiet when things start to go wrong in the experiment reflects their sense of expectations betrayed. I will explore what Milgram's experiment tells us about the operation of power in modern society later in this book.

Milgram conducted a control experiment to test whether people in the teacher role would increase the shocks given to the learner if he allowed them to choose what level of shock to give rather than instructing them to raise the shock level by 15 volts after each question. There was a dramatic reduction of the level of shocks administered. In fact, the shock levels were almost the same at the end of the experiment as at the beginning. Unfortunately, Milgram does not record the number of trials completed by the subjects but it appears that most, if not all of them, completed the experiment. These results indicate that the consequences for the learner are a key factor inducing disobedience and that when there are no serious negative consequences for the learner, participants are happy to oblige the experimenter and carry on administering shocks. These results also indicate that given the opportunity, people use a strategy that allows them to obey the experimenter but not cause harm to the learner. Milgram argues that the results of this condition rule out the idea that people are expressing repressed hostility in his experiments. We know from work in social psychology on de-individualisation that people are more likely to be aggressive if they are in an anonymous setting such as a crowd or if they are in uniform. Allowing participants to choose the level of shock introduces an individualising dimension into the design since people make a choice in which their identity is involved and which reduces their anonymity and increases their sense of personal responsibility.

Milgram then completed a series of experiments in which he varied the actions of the different participants in the experiment. In the different versions of the experiment I have discussed so far the experimenter always gave the commands, so Milgram introduced a condition in which another volunteer instructed the teacher to continue with the experiment and in this condition obedience reduced. Social psychologists draw a distinction between different types of social influence such as commands and requests. In the Milgram experiment, the learner could request that the teacher continue but they could not command them to continue. The obligation implied in a request is not as strong as a command because it is legitimate to refuse a request but not a command given by an authority figure. A request asks the individual to volunteer their action, making the teacher's personal identity and choice salient to them. This variation tells us something else about Milgram's experiment: that the participants were sensitive to the legitimacy of the source of instructions. These results raise interesting questions about the relationship between legitimate authority and power, which I will explore later in this book.

Milgram conducted further variations of this type including using a second confederate to play the role of an apparent third subject in the experiment who, when lots are drawn is assigned the role of the experimenter. An additional twist that Milgram added to this design was to instruct the fake ordinary person playing the role of the experimenter to take over the administration of the electric shocks if the participant wanted to stop the experiment. Under these conditions, there was almost complete disobedience and an increase in the level of protests and complaints from participants. Milgram notes that there were even attempts by some participants in this version of the experiment to restrain the person physically who they thought was another volunteer playing the role of the experimenter from administering shocks. A very effective role variation that Milgram introduced was to swap the roles of the learner and the experimenter on the pretext of demonstrating the experiment. In these conditions, where the experimenter is receiving the shocks and the learner is giving the orders, not a single subject completed the study. These variations indicate that participants' belief that the experimenter is a bona fide researcher is critical to their obedience in the experiments suggesting that authority is most effective when it appears to be official or accredited.

Milgram also made some other variations to his study in which there were two authorities; one played the experimenter as in the other studies while the other was more sympathetic to the learner and suggested that the experiment should stop. All the participants disobeyed in this condition, indicating that the consistency of the authority is critical to obedience. However, I think this result is not simply about the consistency of authority because contradiction between authorities is a strong cue to the participant that there are limits on the power of the experimenter. When given the idea that another authority can legitimately question the experimenter, participants are much more likely to disobey. The first experimenter behaved exactly as he did in the other versions of the experiment suggesting that disobedience may stem in part from a lack of clear authority or confusion about who is in charge. This experiment reinforces the insight that the success of the experiment depends on its separation from the broader social context. Temporarily cutting off contact with people outside the experimental context induces obedience, an effect that diminishes if it is apparent that another authority might question the experimenter.

## Participants' voices

Milgram used deception to create the sense that real consequences followed from participants' actions in the obedience experiments. He believed that when individuals confronted authority in the real world their actions were influenced by the consequences of their choices for them and for others. He was also aware that without these negative consequences there would not be a strong enough motivation to challenge authority. Milgram was critical of previous experiments in social influence because they used situations that did not matter to the participants. In modern societies social influence works in subtle ways, through propaganda, mass mediation, the expression of public opinion, social norms that indicate what is appropriate or not, and through individuals controlling themselves according to norms and rules of conduct. In contrast, in obedience, when an authority figure orders someone to do something, power is made visible, increasing the emotional temperature in the situation and the consequences for the individuals involved.

Milgram used an elegant experimental design to test specific hypotheses with measurable outcomes. He worked hard to make sure his experiment combined relevance with simplicity; that it engaged participants in a believable scenario in which they felt emotionally invested and under pressure. Milgram claimed to have reproduced a power relationship in his laboratory and he knew very well, therefore, that he had to provide evidence that the participants had believed in the experiment. He took care to record the reactions of participants during the experiments using observation, filming the studies and interviewing participants as part of the post-experimental debriefing. He followed this up with a survey of participants a year after the experiments. Here we come up against a paradox in Milgram's thinking which goes to the heart of debates about the use of scientific methodology in social psychology.

Milgram placed great store by the experimental method as a means of testing hypotheses and generating results that would enable him to make strong causal claims about obedience. Yet, at the same time, he was committed to the idea that experiments should be relevant to real life social issues and reflect the experiences that individuals faced in living in the modern world. In addition, he wanted his experiments to provide a useful contribution to understanding the social, political and moral dimensions of the human condition. This is a difficult combination because the key questions of human existence raise complex questions of morality, power, politics and the nature of human experience. Milgram's strategy was to allow his research questions and hypotheses to reflect significant social questions and his deliberations on social, political and moral theory. However, being a strong advocate of the scientific method, Milgram put such philosophical questions aside once the business of experimental design, analysis and interpretation was under way since they had served their purpose in identifying the social issue and in forming the research questions.

In his 1974 book, *Obedience to Authority*, Milgram has two chapters devoted to recording the reactions of participants in the experiments, drawing on what they said during the experiment and in post-experiment debriefing interviews and observations made from filming the experiments. However, because of his faith in science, Milgram saw his experimental results, the number of people who obeyed under different conditions, as his key findings. In contrast, he thought of the qualitative material that he gathered through observations and interviews as useful primarily in demonstrating that the experiment was both realistic and consequential for the participants and provided a picture of the experience of being an obedient subject. Milgram did not present a systematic analysis of his qualitative material but used individual cases to document the variety of responses, reactions and experiences of his participants. The introductions to these case studies reveal something of Milgram's patronising and elitist attitude to his participants:

> The Subject is about fifty years old, dressed in a jacket but no tie; he has a good natured, if slightly dissolute appearance. He employed working-class grammar and strikes one as a rather ordinary fellow (Milgram, 1974, p. 73).

## Participants challenge the experimenter

Notwithstanding Milgram's affected and rather patronising attitude towards his participants, a number of important themes emerge in the case studies of reactions to the experiment reported in his book. For example, one is the importance of the participants' engagement in the experiment as a microcosm, cut off from the outside world. For Milgram's study to work, participants would not only have to accept that the shocks being administered and the responses of the learner are real, but also to suspend their beliefs about the outside world and to desist from interrogating the experiment too closely in terms of the legal and moral codes of their society. They have to believe that there is no way out of the situation and that there is no alternative authority to the one facing them in the laboratory.

Some of the participants' responses reveal challenging the experimenter and disobedience related to thinking about the broader social context. In one example, a participant responds as follows to the suggestion that he has no alternative but to continue with the experiment:

If this were Russia maybe, but not America (Milgram, 1974, p. 48).

This is a lovely quote because it illustrates that to continue with the experiment participants have to suspend their beliefs in the social and legal norms of their society and act as if they are living in a totalitarian state, which this participant is not prepared to do. What is intriguing is that this participant does not question the 'reality' of the experimental set up; he clearly buys into the reality of the shocks and the response of the learner, but challenges the right of the experimenter to implement the experimental procedure. However, participants do challenge the meaning of the experimental context in a variety of ways. An example from the same participant involves a reference to the human rights of the learner indicating that awareness of the rights of the victim provides a reason for disobedience because it appeals to a legal authority outside the experimental context. In the post-experiment interview the same participant indicates that he is religious and that causing harm to others violates religious ethics. Milgram suggests that although the participant disobeys the experimenter, his conduct is still an example of obedience to authority because one authority substitutes for another. However, this seems to me to miss the point that this participant is placing himself outside of the context of the experiment and using an alternative principle with which to counter the claims to authority of the experimenter as a basis for disobedience. This demonstrates that Milgram focused mainly on obedience, even to the point of interpreting disobedience as a kind of obedience. I will revisit the theme of the relationship between authority and dissent at various points in the book.

The story of the Eichmann trial was salient to some participants, indicating that individuals were aware at some level of the link between the questions that Eichmann's trial was raising in the public imagination about the role of individuals in the Holocaust and Milgram's experiment:

As my wife said, 'you can call yourself Eichmann' (Milgram, 1974, p. 54).

This quote indicates that some participants in the experiment challenge the ethics of the procedure and are aware of the broader context in social, political and moral theory that inspired Milgram's experiment; in this case, they ask whether the conduct of individuals would reflect obedience in a totalitarian state. Other participants indicated that they had been able to link the experiment to the issues that had surfaced about the operation of the Nazi regime during the Eichmann trial.

## Interaction between the participants and the experimenter

Milgram instructed the experimenter to use an ordered series of prompts in a firm but polite voice in response to questions from the participant:

Prod 1: Please continue, *or*, Please go on.
Prod 2: The experiment requires that you continue.
Prod 3: It is absolutely essential that you continue.
Prod 4: You have no other choice, you *must* go on (Milgram, 1974, p. 21).

In addition, Milgram allowed the experimenter to reassure the participant if they asked whether shocks were painful. Milgram told the experimenter to reassure the learner that no permanent injury would result. If the participant objected that the learner did not want to continue the experimenter was to say that the participant had to carry on with the experiment whether the learner wanted to or not.

Milgram presents a detailed extract from one of the experiments in his 1974 book in which an extended dialogue occurs between the experimenter and the participant. For the most part, the experimenter does an excellent job of using only the cues that Milgram had provided, however, at various points he departs from the script that Milgram had set for him. For example, the participant expresses concern and asks who will take responsibility if something happens to the learner and the experimenter replies: 'I'm responsible for anything that happens to him, please continue' (Milgram, 1974, p. 74). Later in the exchange, the participant asks for confirmation that the experimenter takes responsibility and the experimenter replies unequivocally, 'The responsibility is mine. Correct. Please go on'. In both cases, the experimenter had departed from the script provided by Milgram.

Milgram's analysis of this exchange focuses on the fact that although the participant objected he carried on with the experiment suggesting that this combination of protest and obedience is an example of cowardice. However, there is surely more to the protests and expressions of concern that participants made that tell us important things about relations of power in the experiment. First, it tells us that people were very much seeing the experiment as taking place in the context of a liberal democratic society. If the experiment were taking place, as one participant says, in Russia or Nazi Germany, then challenging authority would have taken on quite a different meaning. It is significant that many participants were vocal in expressing their concern and that although they showed deference to the experimenter this was often deference under protest. Second, the participant is checking that the experimenter has taken into account the risks to the learner and will take responsibility for any harm done to the learner. This kind of challenge makes sense if we think of the participants as putting the experiment in the context of a society in which the rule of law is in play. This is a tactic on the part of the participant since it aims to bring the authority to account.

A similar pattern emerges in the interview that Milgram presents with a nurse who made a series of mild protests but continued to the end of the experiment. When explaining her actions the nurse draws an analogy to hospital procedures:

> If I question the dose of a drug, I can ask the doctor three times; 'is this what you want? Is this the order you want?' And, if he keeps on saying 'Go ahead', and I know this is above the average dose, I may call his attention to the fact that it is too much. It's not that you are better than he is but you can say 'Did you want her to have so much, doctor,' and then you repeat it. Then you still have the right to bring the question up to the supervisor (Milgram, 1974, p. 78).

Milgram analyses this exchange as indicating the complete acquiescence of the nurse to authority both within and outside the experiment. However, it seems reasonable to say that the nurse was referring to the way people play different, complementary roles in a hospital team and that this implies an obligation on the nurse to bring her doubts about things like dosage levels to the attention of the doctor and if the doctor does not listen to report this to the supervisor. In other words, although it is highly coded, the nurse is required as a professional to challenge doctors under appropriate circumstances and to go over their heads if she does not receive a satisfactory response. As with the previous example, this illustrates that in the Milgram experiment the participants interpreted the experiment against the normal expectations of their everyday lives in the context of US liberal democracy. They assumed that there were authorities and processes that were not visible to them but which they felt they could reasonably appeal to and which safeguarded their rights and those of the learner.

These appeals to the experimenter tell us something else about the way that Milgram's participants understood and responded to authority: they were appealing to authority to be responsible and to govern itself. The participants clearly had an understanding of power as legitimate authority accountable under the law, working through consent and under the obligation of self-limitation. They make the reasonable assumption that the university grants authority to and regulates an academic researcher who can continue to exercise that authority because they act in a disciplined and legitimate way. This makes sense of the protests, expressions of concern, and reference to examples of other forms of authority that I have discussed above, in that they were attempts to appeal to power to govern itself, to act with restraint and to be accountable.

All of these examples speak to the idea that although many participants did not feel they could openly disobey the experimenter they nevertheless performed a range of actions that indicated their belief that the power of the authority was limited. This is in stark contrast to the accounts of victims of the Holocaust, who felt in many cases that protest was futile or counter productive and would be met with extreme punishment. This also qualifies Milgram's conclusions that the participants in his experiments be regarded as obedient to authority. Even though they were following the commands of the experimenter, they made their concerns and opposition heard and they tested the authority of the experimenter in a number of ways. This would be much less likely in Nazi Germany where the participant would face a much more serious threat of punishment for such opposition.

These examples also indicate that Milgram did not put enough focus on disobedience in his experiments and did not look at his observations of people's conduct in the experiment and their interview material as qualitative data that was just as important for understanding power, responsibility and participation as the numbers and levels of obedience measured in the different experiments.

## Emotions and disobedience

According to Milgram, the obedient participants in his experiments gave up their autonomy and agency in response to the commands of authority. For example, Milgram reports the experience of one of the participants who brings the experimenter's attention to the anxiety and strain she is experiencing. Milgram is particularly harsh on the participant who he regards as lacking psychological integration and therefore unable to link her compassion and concern for the learner with the idea of disobeying the experimenter. However, there is another possible interpretation of her emotional outburst during the experiment; that it is a way of bringing the seriousness of the situation to the attention of the experimenter. As a public act of communication, the expression of strong emotions is very powerful as it can be interpreted as an authentic expression of concern. The participant is also relying on the idea that the experimenter will take into account her feelings in the conduct of the experiment, indicating a strong belief that authority is at least potentially responsive and responsible. The participant is tactically deploying her emotional reaction in the course of the experiment to communicate to the experimenter that there is a problem with the experiment.

For Milgram this case contrasts with another in which a woman participant remains in control throughout and refuses to continue with the experiment. She does not accept the reassurances of the experimenter and she asserts her own concern about the impact of the shocks on someone with a heart condition. Her emotional disengagement impressed Milgram compared with the previous participant who displayed her feelings but could not bring herself to disobey. Milgram interprets these two participants as representing two different psychological states that the individual can adopt during the experiment. In one, the person retains control, their own identity to the fore and they disobey the experimenter. In the other, the individual becomes emotional, loses a sense of purpose and appears to be more susceptible to the influence of the experimenter. We will return to this idea in the next chapter when we explore Milgram's explanations of his findings.

## Two phases of the experiment

The quantitative results demonstrated that the reactions of the learner, which became audible at 150 volts, were critical in prompting disobedience. This was the point in the experiment when the learner screamed in pain and was often the point at which people disobeyed by pulling out of the experiment. This was the moment when the reality of the situation and the potential harmful consequences to the learner hit home to the participants. It is also a critical moment because it is clearly more difficult to stop after this point, if people did not respond quickly enough to the changing circumstances of the experiment they found it difficult to justify stopping later. Milgram presents his experiment as an incremental increase in shock levels given to the learner by the participant. However, it is clear that his participants saw the experiment in two phases: before and after 150 volts.

## Conclusions

In this chapter, I have outlined the main features of the design and the main results of Milgram's experiments on obedience to authority. The results indicate that when faced with what they see to be a legitimate authority, individuals are inclined to follow commands even when they have doubts or concerns about the consequences of their actions. It appears that many people when asked to harm a fellow human being in a pressure situation are more prepared to trust to authority than their own judgement. Milgram conducted a range of experiments that demonstrate two key findings: that being close to and aware of the victim reduces obedience and that when the experimenter is not present people are disobedient. Obedience is highest when the authority is nearby and the victim is at a distance. An examination of the experiences of participants in the Milgram experiment also raises a range of questions about the experiments and challenges Milgram's interpretations. In fact, the results and Milgram's interpretations raise many questions that are left unanswered: how do we interpret these results on a psychological level and what are the moral, social and political implications of these findings? I will explore these questions in the rest of this book starting with Milgram's attempt to develop a psychological theory of obedience followed by explorations of the reactions of the psychological community, the social and political implications of the findings and contemporary reflections on Milgram's famous studies.

© Al Satterwhite [www.alsatterwhite.com]

# 2 Milgram's Explanation of His Findings

The experiments that Milgram conducted are fascinating in their own right and the results raise important and worrying questions about human agency and responsibility in the face of authority. However, what motivated Milgram to conduct these experiments and how did he interpret the results? In his book *Obedience to Authority*, written ten years after he had completed his experiments, Milgram was able to develop a psychological theory of the results, to reflect on the ideas that had influenced him and to elaborate on the broader social, political and moral context of his research.

In the preface and first chapter of *Obedience to Authority* Milgram reviews the theoretical questions and social concerns that led him to design and conduct his obedience experiments. Milgram does not start with psychological theory but blends sociological analyses of power and authority with enduring concerns about the Holocaust and political concerns about postwar American society. Milgram's acknowledgements give us some clues as to the key influences on his work. The list of authors he cites are from two different academic traditions: research on the social psychology of social influence, including Asch, Lewin and Sherif and a group of writers of social and political theory who influenced the broader intellectual *zeitgeist* in which Milgram and other social scientists of his day started their careers, including Adorno et al. (1950), Arendt, Fromm and Weber.

Milgram starts his discussion with a paradox which he claims is as old as western civilisation; that authority and obedience are necessary for the cohesion and smooth running of society and therefore of tremendous benefit. At the same time, however, under the influence of authority individuals can perform acts that they would otherwise regard as wrong, immoral or evil. This is an important starting point because it suggests that obedience as a basic function of complex societies can be used for both positive and negative ends, and is therefore value neutral. Although

Milgram is interested in sociological and political questions, he places the individual at the centre of his enquiry. When an authority figure asks an individual to do something they disagree with there is a conflict between the individual and society. Milgram sees obedience to authority through the eyes of a social psychologist who is concerned with the relationship between individuals and society.

For Milgram, the dilemma of obedience resists theoretical explanation and instead requires the disinterested view of the scientist to explore how people deal with the moral dilemma presented by obedience in real social situations. If a person is to follow their conscience rather than obey orders then they will have to disobey authority. Milgram designed an experiment in which an authority ordered individuals to do something that they disagreed with in order to examine the circumstances in which they will accept or resist authority. He was convinced that obedience had positive as well as negative consequences and assumed that individuals would value it, so that choosing not to obey and resisting authority would come at a psychological cost. Milgram assumed that his participants, ordinary citizens living in post-war America had unexceptional private lives, bringing up families, holding down jobs, getting on with their neighbours or not. However, these individuals left the privacy of their homes to travel to an institutional setting so although Milgram sampled from a 'normal' population the participants showed up in their public rather than their private identities. Milgram was relying on the idea that his participants would by default conform to norms of appropriate public behaviour which would include not harming fellow citizens with whom they had no quarrel or personal conflict.

One of the most effective aspects of the design of the obedience experiments is that the authority figure appears to be benign at the beginning of the experiment, a research scientist in a prestigious university. Milgram reasoned that contradicting such a figure would go against the value participants would place on following the directions of authority in public contexts. However, as the experiment unfolded and it became apparent to participants that they were part of a situation that resulted in harm to the learner, another personal value, that of respecting and not harming fellow human beings, came into play. The experiment therefore places the participant in a dilemma. If they obey the authority figure they contradict social norms that sanction doing harm to others. However, if they refuse to harm the other person in the experiment then they would be acting against social norms whereby good citizens defer to legitimate authority.

Milgram acknowledges that the experiment creates an unusual social situation, an intensification and distillation of an everyday occurrence of dilemmas between obeying authority and following personal inclinations. At this point, he introduces the Holocaust as an example of an extreme event where public authority requires individuals to put aside their private values to do their duty even when it contradicts their beliefs. Milgram does not see his experiment as a replication of the operation of authority in Nazi Germany, nor is it a replication of decisions that individuals make in their everyday lives. Instead, Milgram assumes that there is, in essence, a set of universal features of obedience that underpin the phenomenon of both legitimate and malevolent authority which can only be isolated in the laboratory. Milgram adopts a forensic, experimental approach in which he manipulates situational factors that might induce obedience in individuals in order to reveal the psychological dimensions of the experience of obedience to a malevolent authority.

As a psychologist, Milgram proposes that people resolve the dilemma of obedience versus conscience by adopting one of two psychological states. Those who are obedient to authority adopt a psychological state in which they stop defining themselves as autonomous beings and suspend their agency by neither seeing themselves as morally responsible for the consequences of their actions nor as the cause of the harm that results. These participants give themselves over to the agency and responsibility of the authority figure. Milgram calls this the 'agentic state'. In contrast, those who were disobedient were in a psychological state of self-consciousness in which they followed the dictates of their own conscience rather than the commands of the experimenter.

Milgram needed three things to work in his experiments to say anything useful about obedience: the situation needed to be a genuine dilemma for the participants, they had to buy into the 'reality' of the suffering of the learner and they had to be voluntary collaborators with the authority rather than coerced, fearful victims of blind obedience. Milgram aims to demonstrate that it is possible for a form of obedience that has negative effects to result from a free individual choosing to cooperate with an authority. The surrender of agency to the authority is also critical because, as we will see, it mimics something essential in the democratic process as well as autocratic authority; the public give power to those in authority through consent. Here is the first hint that Milgram was concerned with the conditions under which American citizens were prepared to give their assent to their political leaders as well as the operations of totalitarian regimes.

The experimental social psychology tradition of research on social influence informed aspects of Milgram's design. Asch (1952) had demonstrated that people were prepared to go against their own judgement under social pressure. The study of social influence established the power of pre-commitment. People find it difficult change what they are doing once they have started to behave in a particular way. The study of persuasion demonstrated that people were more susceptible if they were involved in a role-play rather than just hearing arguments (Janis and King, 1954). Janis acted as an advisor on Milgram's experiments and Asch had employed Milgram as a researcher on one of his projects. Milgram used all these techniques to establish a procedure that would put pressure on his subjects in the context of a moral dilemma that was meaningful to them and in a context in which their actions would apparently lead to severe harm to another human being.

Milgram makes a number of important assumptions that shape his approach to explanation. He assumes that psychological processes, as demonstrated in experimental contexts reveal fundamental or essential aspects of human nature. Milgram was frustrated by the way in which social, moral and political theory appeared incapable of resolving key questions about human agency and the tendency of theory to fall into opposing ideological camps. He summed up these oppositions as being between liberals and conservatives that mapped on to different ideas about the right way to organise society and govern people based on accounts of human psychology. He therefore turned to empirical scientific methods to see if he could find answers to some of the classic dilemmas of political theory: are men free or in chains, are human beings agents or subject to political control? How can we account for the Holocaust as a feature of the modern world? Is a ruling elite the best form of democratic government or would greater participation make for a better society?

Milgram came to the view that it is impossible to settle such questions at a theoretical level alone, demonstrated by the way in which theory led to the continual rehearsal of opposing philosophical positions. Instead, Milgram believed that finding answers to such questions was more likely to come from empirical, scientific research. He believed that properly conducted scientific experiments gave a special window on the world because experimental control allowed for the isolation of causes and effects and is ideologically neutral. Milgram was part of the pragmatist tradition in that he wanted his experimental social psychology not only to be theoretically and ideologically neutral but also to be relevant to the key social, moral and political questions of the day. Milgram asked how we can explain the Holocaust and what implications obedience to authority has for thinking about the best possible arrangements for democratic society?

## Milgram's explanations of his findings in *Obedience to Authority*

In chapter 10 of *Obedience to Authority*, Milgram begins his explanation of the results of the obedience experiments with a restatement of what he considers the basic findings of his research. He argues that disturbing levels of obedience had occurred in the experiments, 'with numbing regularity good people were seen to knuckle under to the demands of authority and perform actions that were callous and severe' (Milgram, 1974, p. 123). Milgram had demonstrated that obedience is a common reaction to authority, that the proximity of the teacher, learner and experimenter affected the level of obedience, reducing social pressure lowers obedience, that people obeyed even when they disagreed with what they were asked to do and found it upsetting. These were the basic facts of Milgram's experiment that called out for interpretation. What do these results tell us about the human condition? At this point Milgram makes an important decision. He does not return to the social, moral and political questions that framed and motivated his research but instead offers a psychological explanation. It is potentially problematic to seek to explain social, political and moral questions as psychological questions. However, Milgram believed that personal problems reflect social issues and those social, political and moral theories make psychological assumptions that are testable.

Milgram starts his search for potential explanations for obedience, which he regards as a widespread predisposition, with biology. He states his assumption that social groups and societies are inevitably hierarchical and that this has its origins in our natural history. He notes that groups of animals often form dominance hierarchies. An important feature of such dominance hierarchies is that challenges to the established order do not necessarily result in injury or death because of the ritualised nature of fight routines and the use of submission cues by the animal lower in the hierarchy. Milgram suggests that the human animal still carries the tendency to challenge but then submit to dominance cues. Milgram gives this a social biological interpretation; that submission has survived because it conferred evolutionary advantage by enabling the smooth functioning of groups and society, stopping social groups descending into chaos. Milgram contrasts the animal kingdom and human society by saying that human authority is mediated by symbols rather than a series of physical confrontations. When the participants entered the experimental context, a hierarchical relationship confronted them that was articulated in the many clues offered in the context of the university and the laboratory. In submitting to commands of the experimenter Milgram's participants behave similarly to animals displaying submission in status hierarchies. However, in humans, the expression of hierarchical position and challenges are symbolic rather than physical displays of aggression.

Le Bon (1999) argues that crowds create a context in which chaotic, uncivilised behaviour occurs and concludes that individuals are civilised but crowds are not. In contrast, Milgram suggests that obedience in the context of a social hierarchy leads to order and coherent social life. Le Bon locates civilisation within the individual whereas Milgram sees it as resulting from social organisation and from individuals playing their roles within a social hierarchy. Milgram argues that the hierarchy is the basic structure of social groups and society and that the complex differentiation of roles in contemporary society results from people occupying different positions within the hierarchy. Milgram attributes the division of labour in modern society and the consequent advances in technology as the result of the functional ordering of society, which depends upon the tendency of human beings to conform, comply and obey commands in a well-ordered social hierarchy.

> We look around at the civilizations men have built, and realise that only directed, concerted action could have raised the pyramids, formed the societies of Greece, and lifted man from a pitiable creature struggling for survival to technical mastery of the planet (Milgram, 1974, p. 124).

Milgram draws on examples from the animal kingdom to reinforce his view that there are enormous advantages to social groups formed as hierarchies of authority and obedience. He uses the analogy of a wolf pack bringing down prey and eating it in turns according to the dominance hierarchy thereby reducing the dangers of fighting over food and reproducing the stable relations of the group.

> The same is true of human groups: internal harmony is ensured when all members accept the status assigned to them. Challenges to hierarchy, on the other hand, often provoke violence (Milgram, 1974, p. 124).

Milgram is not proposing that obedience is an instinct, but that it is a tendency in people that is essential to the smooth functioning of social groups and hierarchies, which would otherwise descend into chaos, anarchy and violence as illustrated by Le Bon's observations of crowds. What this amounts to is a view that when a social system demands obedience and arranges people into hierarchical roles, the basic human tendency is to acquiesce in that social arrangement; human beings are naturally inclined to take their place in authority hierarchies, but if the society does not demand it then we would not necessarily be obedient.

Milgram uses language learning is an analogy for the way that human nature and social organisation interact. Language is so complex that it is unlikely that people learn to understand and speak through imitation or reward. Instead, they must have a natural capacity to learn language that is triggered by engagement with the language community. Milgram argues that in a parallel way, human beings are born with a tendency to be obedient which is cued by commands in the context of a social hierarchy. Just as different languages use different vocabularies so there can be different forms of society, each of which takes the tendency of people to conform and obey and shapes it according to particular social norms supporting a given social structure. The norms will vary according to the nature of the society; some societies will demand absolute obedience and others will operate with norms based on consent and voluntary commitment. What strikes Milgram is that the results of his obedience experiments demonstrate how readily people who live in a liberal democracy based on consent still submit to the demands of a malevolent authority as if the latent potential of individuals to obey adapts to the social context they find themselves in.

We are now getting an idea of Milgram's understanding of the relationship between our biology and our social identities. He argues that there are two elements to human nature in relation to obedience to authority, one of which is part of our biological inheritance and is best understood as a version of the way that animals show submission when they are threatened. However, whether this inherent tendency is realised in passive obedience depends upon the kind of society that the individual is born into. Like many social psychologists, Milgram regards social behaviour as the result of the interaction of nature and nurture. Having opened up the question of the relative influence of biology and society, Milgram does not pursue it further and instead argues that for his purposes, whatever the relative influence of our genetic inheritance and the impact of society upon our sense of self, the main point is that human beings evolved to be able to function in hierarchies.

These ideas about social coherence being dependent upon functional features of social hierarchies were derived from sociological debates in Milgram's time surrounding the structural functionalism of Talcott Parsons. Parsons was the director of the Department of Social Relations at Harvard in which Milgram registered as a PhD candidate in 1954. The Department of Social Relations was a multidisciplinary department that aimed to integrate the work of social and clinical psychologists, sociologists and social anthropologists (Blass, 2004, p. 17). This context clearly had an intellectual influence on Milgram's efforts to combine his interests in social and political theory with his desire to conduct empirical social psychological studies of social action.

When Milgram sat in on Parsons' classes in 1954/5 Parsons was the pre-eminent sociologist in America; he was president of the American Sociological Association in 1950 and his two books, *The Structure of Social Action* (1937) and *The Social System* (1951) had a profound effect on debates about the nature of sociology as a discipline. Parson's writings were influenced by classical social theory, particularly Weber, Durkheim and Pareto whose work is often in conflict. Parsons took the disparate writings of Weber, Durkheim and Pareto and moulded them into a unitary theoretical framework for sociology: structural functionalism. Parsons, like Durkheim before him, used metaphors from biology to analyse society. Both addressed the key problem of how social cohesion is possible in modern industrialised societies given the dispersal of individuals and the highly specialised and different roles that they play and the divergent lives that they lead. In contrast, in pre-modern society people lived in close-knit communities and were less individuated by differential social roles. Parsons argues that modern societies overcame the potentially fragmentary and disorganising effects of social differentiation in much the same way the body links together the organs, which are highly specialised and dispersed throughout the body into a biological system. The organs have different functions: the heart enables the passage of blood through the circulatory system; the lungs enable the transfer of oxygen from the air into the blood stream, and so on. These organs, have different structures, and play different functional roles in the body as a biological system divided into subsystems such as the circulatory system and the respiratory system.

The body, like a modern society, is structurally differentiated into subsystems and different organs, it is functionally integrated as a holistic entity and the subsystems are organised around organs. This functional analysis complements a structural analysis of the physiology of the organs and a classification of the parts of the body as taxonomy. Functionalism in sociology uses this view of the body as a metaphor for the way that society is organised: structurally different groups and institutions of a complex modern society connected together to provide social cohesion. One of the key principles of systemic organisation of institutions in society is social hierarchy. Milgram interprets the interaction between the experimenter as an authority and the participant as a subject as a moment in the communication between representatives of different subsystems of society which are coordinated through the mechanism of authority.

Alongside structural functionalism in sociology, Milgram was also strongly influenced by the way that cybernetics attempted to formalise the principles of organisation of systems such as the body or society. Cybernetics is the study of the organisational forms that systems need to take to interact with each other. Sociologically, this means treating the individual as a subsystem embedded in a broader social system. Milgram regards the relationship between authorities and subjects as one system seeking to constrain another system. In this case, the social system seeks to constrain the individual system by a control mechanism (issuing orders) which triggers a mechanism in the individual (obedience) which coordinates individual behaviour and the needs of social hierarchy:

> The presence of conscience in men, therefore, can be seen as a special case of the more general principle that any self-regulating automaton must have an inhibitor to check its actions against its own kind, for without such inhibition, several automata cannot occupy a common territory (Milgram, 1974, p. 128).

Milgram thought of conscience as a self-regulatory mechanism that may conflict with the demands made upon the individual by society. He thinks of the individual in a social context as a relatively autonomous bio-psychological system in feedback relationships with other agents as part of a hierarchically arranged system. He linked the self-conscious individual to the autonomous, self-regulating individual and obedience to the connection between the individual and society as a system of authority:

> ... when the individual is working *on his own*, conscience is brought into play. But when he functions in an organizational mode, directions that come from the higher-level component are not assessed against the internal standards of moral judgement (Milgram, 1974, pp. 129–130).

In other words, moral reflection relates to self-control within the person, and authority requires individuals to suspend their moral self-control so that they can meet the organisational needs of the system. Milgram refers to Nazi Germany as an example of a strong hierarchical organisation with the implication that in such a system, moral responsibility resides at the apex of the hierarchy and everyone else in the system suspends their moral judgement in favour of following orders (the agentic state).

Milgram continues with the systems theory analogy to explain why it is that obedience to authority results in widespread social conformity. Mass conformity brings enormous benefits to human beings because a social system of hierarchical control works most efficiently if all the sub-units behave in the same way. Milgram explains this with the analogy of a train braking system, which requires each carriage to stop at the same speed, otherwise they would crash into each other. According to this thinking, social control requires the suppression of difference amongst the population being coordinated, and the more hierarchical a society is the more similarity is encouraged amongst the public. The functional needs of social systems impinge on the individual by making them suspend their self-control in favour of obeying orders for the greater good of the group, institution or society, and this is coordinated through a chain of authority.

Milgram then turns his attention to what the individual has to do to adapt to these requirements placed upon him or her by social organisations. Milgram introduces a new terminology to describe two different psychological states: one referring to self-conscious and morally autonomous individuals he terms 'the autonomous state'; and the alternative, in which people give up their autonomy and moral conscience and are obedient to authority he calls 'the agentic state'. This was perhaps an unfortunate choice of terms because 'agentic state' appears to imply that the individual is an agent but what Milgram means is that they are under the control of an external agent, in this case the experimenter. He suggests that individuals undergo an 'agentic shift' when they move from the mode of being self-conscious individuals to being members of a social group or playing a role in a social situation or institution. Having established the idea that obedience results when individuals shift from a psychological state of self-control to an agentic state in which they are guided by social demands, Milgram explains how social context influences the switch to the agentic state.

## Applying the theory to the experiments

Milgram realises that explaining the agentic state and its relation to autonomy is critical to interpreting the behaviour of participants in the obedience to authority experiments and he explores the conditions that give rise to the agentic state, the behaviours and experiences that arise from the agentic state and the binding factors that keep a person in the state. The critical psychological question in obedience to authority is whether the individual experiences a situation as an autonomous individual or as a social agent (in the agentic state). He is convinced that there is a tendency for individuals to switch into the agentic state when given orders and that this tendency is triggered and maintained by specific features of social situations.

### Antecedent conditions

Under the heading of 'antecedent conditions' Milgram discusses the factors that have shaped the psychology of his participants and which lead them to have a tendency to adopt the agentic state and obey commands. He adopts Parsons' idea that socialisation both in the family and through education establishes a pattern of conformity and obedience in the developing person. Parents discipline and train the child to obey and the school is 'an *institutional system of authority*' (Milgram, 1974, p. 137).

Additionally, in an idea also taken from Parsons, the social system of authority is supported by rewards for those who acquiesce and punishment or sanctions against those who do not conform. Socialisation by authoritarian parents, the obedience required at school and at work and the system of social sanctions imposed on those that do not conform set the general conditions in which individuals' natural inclination to submit turns into obedience in modern society. Milgram suggests that in concrete social situations a set of specific situational factors at the point of command reinforce the effect of the broader culture of conformity. For example, the perceived legitimacy of authority is an important condition leading the subject into the agentic state. The perceived legitimacy of an authority is not dependent on personal characteristics (as in Weber's theory of charismatic leadership) but on the person occupying a role that gives them the legitimate authority to issue orders (e.g. a parent in the family or a teacher in a school).

Individuals entering Milgram's laboratory were inclined to conform because of their immersion in systems of social control all their lives so that they were primed to look to see who is in charge in a given social context. The experimenter in the obedience to authority studies adopted this position by taking the initiative, guiding action and interaction and outlining the rules of the social situation. In addition, the context created by the laboratory, the uniform of the experimenter and the lack of a competing authority established the credibility of the experimenter as an authority figure. Milgram also claims that the fact that the participants were volunteers makes an important contribution because volunteering establishes a commitment to the success of the social situation, which places moral obligations upon participants. In addition to establishing the authority of the experimenter, the experimental context is required to create a coherent sense of reality and link the authority figure and the participant in a credible way so that the authority would be perceived by the participants as entitled to give orders to them. Deception plays an important role in the experiment because it gives a plausible account of the legitimate authority of the experimenter over the subject that is relevant to the social context.

In addition to these situational factors, the authority has to fit in with the participants' broader perceptions and expectations of authority. This is where the scientific setting of the laboratory and the aims of scientific enquiry played an important part in establishing the experiment as the kind of context in which obedience might be expected. In addition, the experimenter provided a rationale for obedience through the contribution that the individual will make to a respected social institution:

> The experimenter acquires his capacity to influence behaviour not by virtue of the exercise of force or threat but by virtue of the position he

occupies in a social structure. There is general agreement not only that he *can* influence behaviour but that he *ought* to be able to. Thus his power comes about in some degree through the consent of those over whom he presides (Milgram, 1974, p. 143).

Here the influence of Milgram's early career in political science comes to the fore in the links between moral obligations of leadership, the institutional setting of government and in the importance of legitimacy and consent. This quote emphasises that what is at stake for Milgram in the obedience experiments is really a question of power; of conditions under which one agent can influence the actions of another and that social influence works by establishing moral obligations for the participant.

## The agentic state

Having offered an interpretation of how the long-term influence of society on the individual combines with features of the experimental context to cause participants to adopt the agentic state and conform, Milgram develops his account of the agentic state. He describes the general characteristics of the agentic state as a narrowing of focus and attention on the task in hand and on the instructions of the experimenter so that other features of the scene (such as the suffering of the learner) are bracketed off; the participant feels themselves 'tuned in' to the authority figure. Milgram draws on the tradition of Mead (1934) and Goffman (1959) at this point to suggest that participants adopt the definition of the situation presented to them by the experimenter with the consequence that obedience follows as a logical consequence of the experimenter's view of the situation. These features of the agentic state affect the moral disposition of the participant in that they feel responsible *to* the experimenter rather responsible *for* the situation. The participants do not experience themselves as immoral but as following a morality of duty, loyalty and discipline. They feel that their actions are a response to the commands of the authority figure and not caused by their own desires or concerns.

Compared to Le Bon's analysis of crowds, in which the individual loses their identity in the flow of energy and activity in the crowd, in Milgram's experiment, the participants give themselves over to a series of orders delivered in a calm, rational manner by an authority figure. Le Bon is concerned with a process of social influence that works through emotions in the social body. Milgram is interested in something different: the enrolment of individuals in a process of rationalisation reflected in the academic and scientific setting and the conduct and demeanour of the experimenter. However, behind the apparent calm of the laboratory setting is something disturbing, reflecting the way that individuals in Nazi Germany were persuaded by an extreme ideology to give up on their individuality to become part of an oppressive collectivism. For Milgram these were not just questions of history but were a reflection on the political culture of the US in the 1950s:

> In growing up, the normal individual has learned to check the expression of aggressive impulses. But the culture has failed, almost entirely, in inculcating internal controls on actions that have their origin in authority (Milgram, 1974, p. 147).

This is a surprising thing for someone to be writing in 1973 after years of violent protests against authority all over the Western world. How could one write this having witnessed the anti-Vietnam War protests and violent demonstrations in support of civil rights in the US, the widespread changes in social conduct of the sexual revolution and the diminishing impact of tradition and authority that accompanied the life political movements? 'The Person is Political' was one of the slogans of the 1960s that brought political apathy into question and demanded political recognition for individual rights. Milgram did refer to atrocities committed by US forces against civilians in the Vietnam War because he thought this supported his argument about destructive obedience. However, he failed to mention the worldwide protests against the Vietnam War and the broader social movements associated with the peace movement, the feminist movement and the human rights movements. This demonstrates that Milgram took a particular political position. He was concerned and critical about the potential of conformity to reduce the accountability of authority in post-war political culture but his critique was a liberal rather than a radical one and could not take on board the radical changes that swept through American political culture and social life during the 1960s.

## Binding factors

Milgram acknowledges that many of the participants did not simply switch into the agentic state when instructed by the experimenter but were in fact profoundly troubled by the conflict between conscience and obedience.

Critically, however, although many participants were upset and expressed their concerns to the experimenter they still obeyed orders. Other participants carried out the orders of the experimenter to the end without feeling the need to question what was going on. What held these participants to the will of the experimenter as the experiment proceeded? They may have been brought up to respect and obey authority but surely, once the negative consequences of their obedience were clear they might have acted differently. Milgram approaches this question by examining what the person has to go through to stop the experiment and openly disobey authority. He acknowledges that the way the experiment is set up, with low-level shocks at the beginning that very gradually increase over time, creates a particular set of circumstances that make it difficult for the participant to stop. The actions required of them are the same at the beginning, middle and end of the experiment (ask questions, give a shock if the answer is wrong, increase the voltage by 15 volts for the next question), but the consequences of the action vary enormously. Therefore, the justification for stopping cannot be an objection to the task itself but to the consequences of the action for the learner, making refusal in the later stages of the experiment difficult because the actions of the participant do not change during the experiment, only the consequences for the learner. The graduated increase in voltage is like being subject to a 'foot in the door' technique of persuasion, which is hard to resist because the difference between the next step and the current one is so small (always just a 15-volt increase in the case of the Milgram experiment). It is as though the early part of the experiment establishes a social contract between the participant and the experimenter so that the participant has to break the contract if they are to follow their conscience later in the experiment.

## Strain and disobedience

An important feature of the obedience experiments was that participants found them upsetting and disturbing; they were under stress. Milgram argues that those who disobey do so because they feel a strain between their role as autonomous individuals and the consequences of playing a role in a relationship of obedience. The obedience experiments put people under pressure to choose between two forms of disobedience: to their conscience and views about appropriate behaviour or to the authority figure.

Strain or the stress resulting from empathy for the harm caused to the learner is incompatible with the agentic state and obedience to authority. The agentic state is focused, instrumental and emotionally detached. Emotional response to the plight of the learner evoke a psychological state that is part of individual identity and therefore 'breaks the spell' of the agentic state, making people aware of their own reflections and concerns about the situation they are in. As the experiment continues a cycle of actions and reactions ensues: The administration of a shock → the learner expresses distress → emotional reaction in the teacher → individual identity more salient in the teacher → expressions of concern from the teacher to the experimenter → experimenter repeats instructions/prompts → learner returns to the agentic state → administration of next shock.

The agentic state, although induced successfully in the laboratory, can be disturbed by thoughts and feelings that are part of the autonomous individual self. If the agentic state does not totally absorb the individual then their sense of themselves as individuals surfaces and comes into conflict with expectations in the experiment. Milgram suggests that there are many thoughts that an individual might have in the obedience experiments that would lead them to disobey. The cries of pain from the learner might cause a sympathetic reaction that reminds the participant that they are a human being. Some participants may have deeply held humanist or religious beliefs that oppose causing harm to others. The participants might be frightened by the possibility of retaliation by the learner and so be reminded that they are a human being who can experience fear and be distracted from the agentic state. The learner makes direct appeals to the participant, which may clash with their sense of duty to the experimenter. The dissonance between individuals' self-images and the callous nature of the task of being the teacher might cause them strain that in turn distracts them from the agentic state. Yet, as we have seen, despite the many ways in which individuals might be 'reminded of themselves', causing them stress, many of them still obeyed the commands of the experimenter.

## Conclusions

Milgram uses a wide range of theories and concepts in developing his research questions, in designing his experiments and in interpreting his results. His thinking ranges from abstract considerations of social and political theory, engagement with sociology, ideas from the social psychology of social influence and concepts from biological and evolutionary psychology. Milgram sees these different levels of explanation, the sociological and the microsociological, the social psychological and individual psychological as interconnected. He believed that an important social phenomenon such as obedience to authority is best understood by looking across these different dimensions of the individual and the social world. Social behaviour, on this view, occurs in the interstices of the social system and individual psychology. A hierarchical social system establishes the conditions in which obedience contributes to social coherence, social situations bind agents into relations of authority and obedience to authority is a social interaction between the authority and the subject. The individual responds to authority by adopting one of two psychological states of autonomy or engagement. Milgram's approach has much to commend it: a multidisciplinary approach, engagement with theories at different levels of abstraction, his connection with social and political theory, and the combination of experimental and phenomenological methods and analysis. Despite these strengths, the academic community has raised many questions and objections to Milgram's method, analysis and theory, which I will review in the next chapter. In addition, the findings and Milgram's discussion raise many questions related to power, political subjectivity, morality and the continuing relevance of the experiments, which I will examine in subsequent chapters on the sociological and political dimensions of these obedience experiments.

# 3 The Reaction of the Psychology Community

## The controversy surrounding Milgram's obedience experiments

Milgram's obedience studies are among the best-known psychology experiments and have been widely discussed in other academic disciplines and amongst the public. However, the studies were deeply controversial amongst the psychological community for a variety of reasons: some challenged the quality and design of the experiments themselves, many were concerned about the ethics of the experiment and there were questions over Milgram's interpretations of his findings. In this chapter, I will look at these problems and issues identified by psychologists in response to Milgram's studies.

Caryl Marsh (2000) tells a story that illustrates the reactions provoked by the Milgram experiments within the psychological community. The American Psychological Association celebrated its 100th anniversary in 1992 and marked the event with a number of conferences, meetings and publications. As part of the celebrations, the association organised an exhibition of examples of the best psychological research of the previous century. A number of venues hosted the exhibition across the US including the prestigious Smithsonian Institute in Washington DC. Milgram's obedience experiment was chosen as one of the featured exhibits, apparently confirming its status amongst the most well-known and important psychological studies of the twentieth century. The organisers retrieved Milgram's original shock generator from the archives of the history of American Psychology and made it the centrepiece of the exhibit. The display was a creative construction. Visitors entered via a covered corridor paved with black and white square tiles. Signs above the entrance and along the walls of the 14-foot corridor asked people to walk only on the black tiles (Marsh, 2000, p. 148). At the end of the corridor, there was a glass display cabinet holding the shock generator and the accompanying script, which invited visitors to reflect on why they had followed the instructions to walk on the black squares only. The script presented examples of obedient social behaviour such as queuing in shops or crossing the road at designated crossing points and included Milgram's account of the ubiquity of obedience to authority as a possible explanation for the results of the experiments. Also included was a short description of the prototype procedure of the Milgram experiment along with the headline figure of the $^2/_3$ of people who administered the maximum shock level.

Visitors were then told that since Milgram's day stricter ethical standards had been put in place in psychology to monitor experiments like Milgram's, particularly the ethics of deceiving experimental participants and leaving them ignorant of the purposes of the experiment, so that it would now be impossible to conduct the Milgram experiments in the way that he did. The exhibit ended with a viewing area playing the original film made by Milgram of his experiment and other classic experiments in social influence. Philip Zimbardo provided a voiceover. Zimbardo is an eminent social psychologist who also conducted a controversial study on social influence when he converted the Stanford Psychology department into a setting for a prison role-play experiment. In the Zimbardo experiment, student volunteers played the roles of prison guards and prisoners in an extended role-play. The experiment had to be terminated because the participants took their roles so seriously that there were incidents of cruelty and abuse from guards and those playing the role of prisoners suffered psychological problems. Zimbardo's prison experiment raised similar doubts about the ethics of social psychological experiments that surrounded Milgram's work and brought equal measures of notoriety and attention.

Marsh (2000) discusses the strong opposition amongst some psychologists to the inclusion of Milgram's work in the exhibition. She reflects that as part of her own training as a psychologist she had noticed the idea that the Milgram experiment was objectionable on ethical grounds, that Milgram's interpretation of his results was questionable and that the experiments were considered an embarrassment by many psychologists. Some psychologists argued that the controversial and problematic nature of the experiment should lead to its exclusion from a public exhibition celebrating the best of American Psychology. However, Marsh recounts that other psychologists supported Milgram's work and the inclusion of the obedience studies in the exhibition, among them social psychologist Roger Brown who spoke out on Milgram's behalf with the result that the exhibit, electric shock generator and the explanation of the headline findings were included in the centenary exhibition.

In her reflections on the exhibition, Marsh discusses the reactions of visitors. The Milgram exhibit was amongst the most memorable for visitors, reinforcing the idea that Milgram's experiment is arresting and interesting. However, reactions were split between those fascinated by the results of the experiment and those upset by even the relatively mild experience of finding that they had conformed by standing on the black squares. The information presented at the end of the walkway featured the baseline condition of Milgram's experiment in which two thirds of people obeyed to the maximum degree by finishing the study and administering 450 volts. The implication is clear and unsettling: that conforming by standing on the black squares suggests that you as an individual would have been amongst those who completed the Milgram experiment and were prepared to hurt another person when asked to do so by an experimenter. Those of us who have lectured on the Milgram experiment will have had the experience of asking for a show of hands from our students, would they disobey the experimenter? When asked the question, most of the students' hands go up and when asked about this they say that they could not imagine complying with authority and harming another person even in a psychology experiment.

These reactions indicate why some in the psychological community have severe reservations about the Milgram experiment and these were collected together and reviewed in 1986 in an excellent book by Arthur G. Miller called *The Obedience Experiments: A Case Study of Controversy in Social Science*. Miller suggests that the many commentaries, criticisms and reflections on Milgram's experiments lead to three major concerns: the ethics of the experiments, the methods used in the experiment and Milgram's interpretation of his results. Milgram was involved in these debates himself defending both the ethics of his research and the validity of the studies as well as developing his theoretical interpretation, all of which shaped the writing of the second half of his 1974 book *Obedience to Authority*.

## The ethics of the obedience experiments

Milgram admits that his experiment involves participants in a situation that is troubling and upsetting. Milgram's own observations, the follow-

up interviews and the films of the experiment all confirm that many participants were confused and emotionally disturbed by the experience. The
strain that the participants were under during the experiment is visible in
the film that Milgram recorded during the experiments. Participants are
visibly hesitant, upset, angry and frightened. These strong reactions of
participants are enough in themselves to raise questions about the ethics
of the Milgram experiments, but they also prompted psychologists to look
critically at Milgram's procedure since participants were both distressed
and deceived.

The scientific community was not slow to notice these ethical issues.
Diana Baumrind (1964) wrote a paper outlining her reaction to Milgram's
first academic paper in which he reported the findings from his initial procedure. Her paper articulates the misgivings that some psychologists had
about the ethics of the obedience experiments. Baumrind reflects on the
relationship between experimenters and public participants and contrasts
the idea of the 'duty of care' that the experimenter should have towards
the participants and the way that volunteers were treated by Milgram.
Baumrind argues that a tension existed between Milgram's ambition as a
scientist and the need to take care of his participants. She argues that
researchers should take particular care over the design and procedure of
experiments that potentially cause harm to participants.

Baumrind is also concerned that the design of Milgram's experiment
reflected his desire to see how social influence would work in an experimental context in which the participants would feel that something was
at stake. The design of the experiment commits the participant, encouraging their sense of involvement as well as pressurising them through
instructions. Milgram wanted the participants to feel that their actions in
the experiment mattered, so he left no doubt that the learner was experiencing discomfort and pain because of the shocks that the participants
administered. Baumrind argues that Milgram should have used special
measures, including clinical assessment of participants and support for
those who have stressful or upsetting experiences given that distress was
a potential outcome of involvement in the obedience experiments.

In addition to raising these points about the ethics of care that Milgram
owed his participants, Baumrind suggests that there is a particular breach
of trust involved in Milgram's procedure. She suggests that there are a
special set of ethical concerns in play because the natural attitude of participants as volunteers is that they are there to help the experimenter to

contribute to scientific knowledge; they approach the experiment in a passive and respectful way, which makes them particularly susceptible to Milgram's manipulations. Baumrind is also concerned about Milgram's style of writing; she suggests that his attempts to use the objective voice of the scientist leads to a lack of empathy both towards his subjects in the conduct of his research and in his descriptions of their reactions in his writings. This criticism anticipates what would become a stronger criticism of psychological research from a feminist perspective and suggests that the objective voice of science reflects the male position of objectifying the world rather than aiming to understand it.

The final point that Baumrind makes is that the potential harm to participants in Milgram's experiments can only be justified if the potential gains to knowledge are high. She draws a comparison with the weighing of medical advances against risks in trials on human subjects in medical research. Baumrind suggests that researchers in the human sciences should act with caution because there are always doubts about the value of research. This complicates the arguments about the ethics of research because by its nature, social scientific research, even experiments like Milgram's, are not capable of the levels of control exercised in natural science and the implications of the results often require debate and interpretation. The value of the research in the social sciences cannot often be judged using objective measures equivalent to the effectiveness of a drug or the number of lives saved by a new treatment. Baumrind advocates a precautionary principle: there are always limitations to social scientific research arising from indeterminacies of theory and method so researchers should always err on the side of caution and not assume that their results will ever be robust enough to justify harming human subjects.

Milgram wrote a response to Baumrind, also published in *American Psychologist* in 1964. He agrees that the procedure upset and distressed some of the participants in his experiment, but still defends his experiment as ethical on a number of grounds. He draws an ethical distinction between experiments that deliberately set out to induce stress in participants and those which unintentionally cause distress. Milgram claims that he did not design his experiment to induce stress, nor did he anticipate the high levels of obedience in the experiment. The distress experienced by participants was, therefore, an unanticipated and unintended consequence of the experimental design. Milgram suggests he has strong evidence for this in his findings that experts and lay people did not predict the outcome of the experiments.

This defence is problematic because Milgram did intend many features of the design of the experiment to apply pressure on the participants, which clearly contributed directly to their stress and emotional upset. For example, the graduated increase in voltage level committed participants to responding when the consequences are low and slowly turned this into a situation where the consequences are high. In addition, Milgram himself argues that participants were placed in a situation of conflict where they had to decide to do one of two negative things (disobey their conscience or disobey an authority figure), and dilemmas of conscience played out in public are potential causes of stress. Furthermore, the role of the experimenter was designed to apply pressure on the participants to continue and not to give them an easy way out of the situation. More broadly, the context of an experimental laboratory places the participants in a vulnerable social role where their natural subject position is to play a relatively passive and supportive role and to trust the experimenter, and they have to overcome this presumption to disobey. The main aim of the study was to measure obedience but to achieve this Milgram designed an experiment that worked by exerting a range of pressures on the participant that made it hard to disobey.

The other reason why Milgram's defence appears disingenuous is that one of his main motivations in designing the study was to put the participant in a situation that would matter to them. He had particularly criticised previous experiments in social influence for not placing the participants in a situation which had consequences and put two core values (autonomy and obedience) in conflict, thus forcing them to face up to that conflict in a lose-lose situation. Milgram designed his study to do both of these things and it seems strange for him to argue that he did not intend his participants to feel stressed! As if to acknowledge this point, Milgram maintains that it is necessary to take risks (including risking the harm of participants in experiments) in order for science to advance. This misses many of the points made by Baumrind that Milgram had a duty of care beyond that of the normal experiment. Given the potential harm to participants there were things that could have been done to support them more effectively, such as involving a clinical psychologist. It also seems right to say that Milgram had a duty to justify the value of his findings more clearly than would normally be the case given the risks to participants. The psychology community was to side more with Baumrind than with Milgram and, partly in response to the controversy surrounding Milgram's experiment, much tighter ethical controls are now a normal part of research practice in psychology. For example, deception is unethical because it potentially affects the relationship of trust involved in human experimentation and therefore requires strong and explicit justification. However, although these restrictions on the use of deception are in place, the American Psychology Association and the British Psychology Society both accept that carefully managed deception is still an acceptable and important experimental tool. This is because deceit enables researchers to examine phenomena potentially invalidated by participants knowing the purpose of the study.

Milgram makes a lot of the fact that neither he nor the other people he asked anticipated the results before the experiments. However, this complicates the issue of consent because Milgram has effectively demonstrated that individuals are not able to predict the outcome of the experiment and therefore are not in a position to give informed consent. If Milgram had asked them before the experiment whether they would harm others by giving electric shocks they would have said no, but Milgram's results indicate that this is not a reflection of how most people will behave in the experiment and demonstrates that the use of deception potentially invalidates consent in psychological experiments. In addition, if participants were obedient in the experiment this contradicted their sense of autonomy, which is a central part of identity that may make people feel guilt and self-criticism for harming another human being. Baumrind suggests that Milgram should have stopped the experiment as soon as it became clear that participants were in distress. In response, Milgram claims that although there were clear signs of distress he took the view that this was not something that would have a long-term effect on the subjects. Here Milgram also appears to be missing the main point because Baumrind links the expression of distress to the idea that participants could come away from the experiment with a sense of shame. It contrast, Milgram persists with the suggestion that there were no long-term effects resulting from participation in the obedience experiments. He cites the case of a letter he had received from one of the participants a year after the experiment, saying how valuable they had found participation in the experiment.

In his responses to Baumrind, Milgram appears not to consider another very well known phenomenon in social psychology, which was one of the main theories of attitude formation and change in Milgram's day: the theory of cognitive dissonance. According to this theory, people will go to great lengths to preserve their sense of themselves as a consistent person. The letters that Milgram received could well be part of self-justification and at the very least indicate that participating in the experiment was something that was still affecting people a long time after the event. Milgram reports the results of a postal survey completed by participants after the study in which people indicated that they were glad to have taken part in the experiment. His interpretation of these findings is again disingenuous, suggesting that this shows that people did not suffer long-term ill effects. However, one of the things that Milgram does not note is that the participants who were 'obedient' were more likely (47%) to say that they were very glad to have participated in the experiment than those who had disobeyed (40%). Self-justification was stronger amongst those who had obeyed the commands of the experimenter, indicating that it did matter to people how they had behaved in the experiment. Milgram's response is also not convincing in that he does not address the central concerns that Baumrind outlines. In particular, he fails to respond to the criticism that the way that briefing and debriefing and follow up evaluation is done in a psychological experiment is not adequate to deal with the selection of vulnerable participants, the lack of emotional and clinical support and the possibility of long-term effects.

In addition to her issues with Milgram's method, Baumrind suggests that given the potential harm that the experiment might do to participants Milgram has to demonstrate the real value gained from the studies. She particularly doubts Milgram's claim in his original paper that the experiments shed light on the Holocaust. In his response, Milgram suggests that the generalisation of his findings is not specific to the Holocaust but addresses general principles of obedience to authority. This is an important argument because Baumrind is right to point out that Milgram explicitly links his study to the Holocaust. However, he claims in his reply that although concerns about and reflections on the Holocaust were salient to him, he regards his experiment as a scientific attempt to isolate factors that influence obedience in a way that reflects general relationships between psychological characteristics of individuals and the social pressure in situations. Milgram does not claim that he is trying to capture the conditions of the Holocaust in the laboratory but that he is trying to isolate factors that affect obedience in the laboratory. Milgram suggests that he introduced the idea of the Holocaust as a 'background metaphor;' in other words an extreme case in which the central importance of obedience to social life is illustrated but that his experiment is aimed at obedience as a general phenomenon. Milgram's point about his aims as a scientific social psychologist is important but many of Baumrind's criticisms appear to have merit. Milgram did not choose to study benign or even positive examples of obedience, his experimental setup does mirror the thesis of banal destructive obedience reflecting the Eichmann trial and Arendt's notion of the banality of evil, and he did use a setup where one authority commands an individual to harm another. The link with the Holocaust looks like more than a background metaphor when we consider these issues, and I will return to this in a later chapter.

At the end of his reply to Baumrind, Milgram gets into a discussion of broader social and political issues and suggests that Baumrind's portrayal of participants as victims of his experimental procedure reflects a negative view of individuals as determined in their behaviour by circumstances and hence as vulnerable and lacking agency. Milgram denies this and suggests that the setup of his experiments assumes that individuals are active social agents capable of exercising choice and self-determination. Milgram also suggests that his broader social motivation is to present findings that will allow the public to reflect on the conditions that potentially create obedience so that they can better assert themselves in the future. Milgram ends his reply to Baumrind with a distinction between two psychologies and suggests that different ethical principles apply to the scientific branch and the therapeutic branch of psychology. Since he is conducting science, he regards himself entitled to observe and manipulate his participants and while he commits to taking due care and diligence of participants, he suggests that those principles of care are different to those that apply to clinical practice and which he thinks have influenced Baumrind's criticisms and concerns.

The debate between Baumrind and Milgram was not the end of the matter; it was the beginning. The high profile of the experiments and the immediate debate between Baumrind and Milgram helped to bring ethical questions in psychological research to widespread attention in the psychological community. As Miller (1986) suggests, their debate covered the main points of the subsequent debate about the ethics of psychological experimentation. These include the question of whether deception is ever justified, the importance of adequate briefing and debriefing and appropriate support, the role of informed consent, the consideration of alternative research methods and the recognition of the needs of vulnerable participants.

The debate between Milgram and Baumrind was timely because it focused on the relation between the rights of the elite institutions of science to gain knowledge and the rights of the individual participants in experiments. In 1964 in the USA, the question of human rights and the power of institutions in society was an important part of the emerging life politics that led to protests and challenges to authority in all its guises. Milgram's experiment, which at first sight appeared to be about historical events in the Holocaust turned out to reflect social issues and changes in American society. The experiments were a microcosm of a transition point in American politics and society. They represented both the old post-war consensus and Cold War context but also anticipated emerging life political issues of the rights of individuals. This context gave new purchase to the realisation that deception was an expression of the different power positions of the scientist and the participant. Kelman (1967) summarises the concern about the increasing use of deception in experimental social psychology with a quote from Vinacke (1954): 'What ... is the proper balance between the interests of science and the thoughtful treatment of the persons who, innocently, supply the data' (Cited in Kelman, 1967, p. 1). Kelman's review demonstrates that deception had become commonplace in social psychological research and that some of the most influential studies in social psychology in the 1950s and 1960s were experiments involving deception. For example, the classic experiments by Festinger and Carlsmith (1959) on cognitive dissonance in which subjects were deceived by being told that the experiment had ended and then asked to assist the experimenter in a task, which turned out to be the experiment proper.

The questions raised by Baumrind were precursors of a much broader set of debates within social psychology, which would ultimately bring into question the role of social psychology in support of the status quo in society and the validity of science as a way of understanding social life. Working in the early 1960s Milgram aimed to educate and inform the public from a position of knowledge and expertise; a position that later generations of social psychologists would bring into question in favour of a more critical and reflective role for social psychology. Milgram's celebration of and trust in the scientific method would also be challenged by later social psychologists as science in general and psychology in particular became associated with power and social control rather than being seen as a source of emancipatory social knowledge.

This tells us something important about the Milgram experiment: that although the findings of the study were fascinating and argued over, there are a range of issues surrounding the experiment itself that go beyond the findings. In this case, it became the vehicle for extended debates on the ethics and social role of psychological experimentation. This also illustrates the creative genius of Milgram. He did not just design a study to extend our understanding of social influence but created a phenomenon. The experiment was like a morality play. The experiment as performance was a vehicle for the public discussion of a range of social, moral and political issues of the day. These issues continue to be relevant today.

The ethics of the obedience experiments are still under debate. For example, Bortolotti and Mameli (2006) use the Milgram experiment to illustrate the potential dangers of deception notwithstanding the use of ethics codes:

> The participants were deceived about the purpose and design of the experiment and about the role of the other participants. Moreover, they were told to follow the instructions despite manifesting uneasiness. The participants were debriefed, at a time when debriefings were not required by the professional codes of ethics, but after debriefing they had to deal with the knowledge that they had been capable, under the influence of authority, of inflicting considerable pain on others (Bortolotti and Mameli, 2006, p. 263).

Milgram, as we have seen, claimed that there was no long-term harm caused to his participants but this is open to doubt. The principle of the violation of autonomy presents more difficulties for the Milgram experiment. He denied the participants their autonomy because they did not have critical information that would have informed them and enabled them to be more in control of the experimental context. The experience of loss of autonomy, might in turn lead to distrust of experimentation in psychology, which will in turn reduce the effectiveness of psychological research. There is no doubt that Milgram compromised the autonomy of his participants. Milgram's response is that, at least in principle, the value of reflection on obedience both for the participants and for the wider public make the loss of autonomy of participants justified.

Bartolotti and Mameli (2006) suggest a positive justification for the use of deception in psychology experiments. They might help individuals to identify behaviours that are habitual, routine or unconscious which have negative effects for them. This knowledge might have positive value if as a result it made people aware of the negative effects of their own behaviour and allowed them to avoid this in the future. Milgram implicitly claims this to be the case; he maintains that the autonomy of individuals in modern societies is compromised by their tendency to be obedient to authority and that his dramatic findings, bringing this tendency into the public domain, will help people to take greater care when they are confronted by authority. He also claims a broader social value for his research by linking to the thesis of the banality of evil and claiming that a more widespread raising of consciousness will make the public bring authority to account and lessen the possibility of widespread blind obedience. This potentially compensates for the lower self-esteem arising from participation in the experiment by making the individual more aware of the impact of obedience in the future. A set of circumstances that threatens autonomy may be upsetting at the time but might provide a good lesson in the value of retaining self-control and independence.

These arguments show that the possible ethical justification for Milgram's experiments lies beyond the experiments themselves and rests on the capacity of individuals and society to learn the lessons of the experiment. Milgram himself offers no such evidence but he did play an active role as a public intellectual in promoting his work to the widest possible audience and challenging the public to take note of his findings and reflect on the immanent dangers of obedience to authority.

## Methodological issues

One of Milgram's basic motivations in his transition from political science to social psychology was his belief in the potential of empirical research to resolve irreconcilable theoretical debates in social, political and moral theory. He also made strong claims about the value of scientific, experimental methods and although he recorded participants' responses and interviewed them, he regarded the results of his experiment as his primary data. However, psychologists were not all convinced by Milgram's experimental design and many of them were sceptical of his broader claims about the validity of experimental methods as a means of answering complex social, moral and political questions. Miller (1986) summarises some of the most important criticisms of Milgram's method by the psychological community.

Psychologists have questioned the validity of the Milgram experiments, casting doubt on whether his study in fact produces destructive obedience. Psychologists question whether the meaning of the experiment for participants was as realistic as Milgram claims (Miller, 1986, p. 140). This is important because if the participants in the experiments did not believe they were really harming the learner then Milgram's interpretations of his results as an example of destructive obedience are invalid. The best-known example of this line of criticism of Milgram's research is Orne and Holland's (1968) paper, which explored what psychologists call 'demand characteristics' in the Milgram experiment. Orne (1962) suggested we should regard human participants in psychology experiments as 'active, curious, and concerned individuals' (Miller, 1986, p. 140). People who volunteer for psychology experiments arrive with expectations concerning their role. For example, they take the experimenter's lead, listen attentively to what they are instructed to do and rationalise their contribution as valuable to the outcome of the study. They assume that the experimenter requests their participation for a good reason even if they are not always clear about the purposes of the experiment. Participation in many psychological experiments is very boring, involving the repetition of simple tasks and even if the participants cannot make sense of the meaning of their actions in the experiment they hold on to the idea that there is some purpose to it and that the experimenter has a good reason for asking them to do what they do. However, although participants make positive assumptions about the ultimate good intentions of the experimenter and value of the experiment, they are also curious and try to work out the purposes and hypotheses of the experiment. Their expectations potentially influence their behaviour in experiments, their trust in the motives of the experimenter, and their view of the purposes of the experiment. This is a problem because the validity of experimental research assumes that the experimental manipulation influences people's behaviour and not the way that the participant interprets the demands upon them in a desire to please the experimenter.

Orne and Holland (1968) argue that the expectations held by participants' influenced their behaviour in the obedience experiments in crucial ways that challenge Milgram's assumptions that they respond in a naturalistic way to his manipulations. Orne and Holland point out two important features of the Milgram experiments: that the experimenter behaved in ways that confounded the expectations of participants (they call this the incongruity effect) and that the subjects may not have believed that they were inflicting pain on the learner. The calm and detached conduct of the experimenter may have moderated participants' responses to the suffering of the learner. They would expect an experimenter to intervene if someone were potentially being harmed in an experiment and because there was no intervention, even when participants directly asked the experimenter to act, they may well have assumed that something strange was going on. Participants may have taken this as a cue that they were in an experiment and could continue playing the role of the dutiful participant. When the participant appeals to the experimenter, ('the person in there is in pain') and the experimenter refuses to shift from their prescribed role, this acts as confirmation that the experiment is a role-play. If the learner was really suffering horribly and dying, then for the experimenter to ignore this they would have to be a psychopath or acting out a role-play; the participants decided it was the latter. Once the participant decides to go along with the experiment, they are likely to keep this up, even in post-experimental interviews when they are still in the role of participant. Ironically, this implies that those who disobeyed were more likely to have believed in the reality of the experiment than those who obeyed (Miller, 1986, p. 146).

Because of the concerns about ethics and the methodological problems in Milgram's experiment, a range of studies within social psychology explore whether role-playing is an alternative method for studying obedience to authority. Kelman (1967) suggests that role-playing can overcome the main objections to Milgram's experiments: the use of deception and the potential lack of trust between experimenters and participants. A number of psychologists conducted role-play versions of the Milgram experiment including Mixon (Mixon, 1972, 1976, 1977). Mixon got students to play out the different roles in the Milgram experiment by acting them out without the laboratory setting and equipment and was able to demonstrate obedience rates similar to those in Milgram's original experiment. Mixon's role-plays suggest that the difference between the estimates of those predicting the results of the experiments and the results of the experiments themselves is due to these different groups (people imagining the experiment and those participating in the experiment) imagining very different experiments. People who reflect on the experiments as observers accept that the conditions are realistic whereas participants regard the experiment as a complex role-play. Based on comments made by his participants Mixon suggests that Milgram's subjects had good reason to doubt that the experiment was real and that they may have realised it was a role-play, did not believe they were harming the learner, and behaved accordingly. In another variation, Mixon told his role-play participants that the learner was not hurt in the experiment and under these conditions; levels of obedience in the role-play matched or exceeded those in the Milgram experiment. Contrary to Milgram's assumptions, knowing, or suspecting that the obedience experiments are a role-play does not reduce obedience and can increase it as participants play out their roles.

The example of role-play in studies of obedience raises an important issue of method, which Harré (1979) terms 'the meaning problem'. The work on demand characteristics and the broader use of role-play in studies of obedience demonstrates the importance of considering the interpretation that participants make of the experiments they are part of since this interpretation makes sense of their behaviour and may well be at odds with the experimenter's views. The role-play studies offer an interesting potential interpretation of the difference between the predictions of how people would behave in the experiments and Milgram's findings. This interpretation reflects the difference between the perspective of the external observer of other people's behaviour and the view of participants engaged in the studies. Role-play appears able to give people an insight into and empathy for the meaning of the experiment for the participants rather than the view of an external 'objective' observer.

## Theoretical reflections on social impact theory

Roger Brown is one of Milgram's most ardent advocates within social psychology; he regards the obedience experiments as amongst the greatest ever conducted in social psychology. In his book *Social Psychology: the second edition*, Brown (1986) describes Milgram's experiments and some of the replications and then discusses two issues that emerge from the Milgram studies: the potential for collective action in response to authority and an interpretation of Milgram's findings using social impact theory. Brown chooses these two themes carefully because the first highlights that Milgram had isolated individuals in his laboratory and the second is an implicit repudiation of Milgram's theory in favour of Latané's (1981) theory of social impact.

Brown draws on a study by Gamson and his colleagues (Gamson et al., 1982) in which individuals in a small Midwest town in the US were contacted by telephone and invited to participate in research conducted by a market research company at the local Holiday Inn. The phone call in which the researcher recruited the participants involved an ingenious form of deception. He first asked if they were willing to participate in four kinds of research: Brand recognition research; product safety research; research in which they would be misled about the purpose until afterward and research involving group standards (Brown, 1986, p. 11).

If a participant agreed to take part in the study, the researcher told them that of the four kinds of research they had agreed to participate in the one that was running now was research involving group standards. The researchers took the view that by agreeing to the full list the participants had implicitly given their permission to be misled. Of course, participants were misled about being misled!

Brown (1986) then describes the procedure. Participants were told to report to the Holiday Inn and met by a smartly dressed researcher (an academic playing the role of a market researcher) who explained the purpose of the study they had agreed to be involved in. Following Milgram, the experimenters designed a scenario that would be both realistic and meaningful to the participants by asking people to engage in a study of the development of group or community standards. An important feature of both the Milgram experiment and Gamson's is a seriousness of purpose. Gamson achieved this by informing his participants that the market research company was collecting the views of concerned citizens using group discussions in order to help a court to have an idea about community standards to decide on cases involving questionable morals. Nine participants congregated in a room that had a U-shaped table with nine seats, each with a microphone and three video cameras to record the discussion. The participants were met by a coordinator who was in charge of proceedings and his assistant who started by distributing questionnaires asking for participants' attitudes on a variety of social issues such as workers' rights, attitudes to large corporations and extramarital affairs. Participants also filled out a form giving their permission to be filmed and acknowledging payment (Brown, 1986, p. 12).

The coordinator then read out a statement that described a legal action taken by an individual (Mr C) who had recently had his franchise to run a petrol station revoked by the parent company. The oil company had hired a private investigator who had discovered that Mr C was living with a younger woman and the company, advised by its lawyers had concluded that Mr C was morally unfit to be their representative in his community and had therefore terminated his franchise agreement. However, Mr C had been publicly critical of the companies pricing strategies and was convinced that the investigation and subsequent revoking of his franchise was a response to his criticism of the company and that his morals and lifestyle were being used as an excuse (Brown, 1986, pp. 12, 13).

The coordinator then asked the group to have a short discussion of the issues in the case, which he informed them that he would record, and then retired to an adjacent room. After a while, the coordinator returned and instructed the group to have another discussion but this time he asked three of the nine participants to role-play the position of offended local citizens and argue against Mr C. The researchers switched the cameras on and the coordinator left the room returning to set up a third discussion and to instruct six individuals to argue on behalf of the company. Following these group discussions, the researcher recorded individual interviews in which participants played the role of individuals in the community offended by Mr C's conduct. Finally, the researcher asked participants to sign an affidavit giving permission for the potential use of tapes made during the experiment in court (Gamson et al., 1982).

All but one of the groups protested strongly against the procedure, refusing to sign the permission at the end of the study and often voicing their concerns in strong or aggressive terms. In fact, the emotional climate of the groups became so intense that Gamson had to stop the study less than halfway through the planned 80 trials. These results appear to contradict Milgram's findings in that here the majority of participants disobeyed whereas in the Milgram study the majority obeyed. Brown interprets this as resulting from the fact that the individuals were not isolated in the Gamson experiment and that the study demonstrates the potential of collective action to bring authority to account.

We can agree with Brown's interpretation that the presence of others strengthened the resolve of individuals to disobey authority. However, there are some caveats. A critical difference between the Milgram experiments and the Gamson study is the presence of the authority figure. Remember that when Milgram conducted studies in which the experimenter left the room there was a radical drop in the levels of obedience. The role of the experimenter and the coordinator were different in the two studies in that the prompts given by the experimenter in the Milgram experiment, with the experimenter standing over the participant and prompting whenever there was hesitation, were an important component of obedience. Further, Gamson's study actively invokes a court of law, which is an important authority outside the experimental context. The social isolation of the participants and the design involving a single authority are important features of Milgram's obedience experiments. Protest and disobedience in the Milgram experiment often took the form of invoking an external authority and referring to the context beyond the laboratory. All of these features were critical to the obedience in the Milgram experiment and we have seen that when Milgram varied these conditions obedience reduced dramatically. Brown's argument illustrates the problem of only using the famous first Milgram procedure as his point of comparison.

The theoretical purposes to which Brown puts the comparison of the Milgram and Gamson studies is also interesting. Brown suggests that the studies give us insight into human behaviour under different social conditions that mirrors mechanics in physics and allow psychologists to develop general laws of social forces. This is quite different to Milgram's conception of scientific social psychology. Social psychologists, working as they do in the interstices of sociology and psychology, often doubt whether they have a credible sphere of reality to which to apply their theories and concepts. Social psychology is the study of the interaction between individuals in groups or between individuals and social institutions and therefore falls between the epistemological assumptions of psychology and sociology. Social psychology studies ephemeral moments of social interaction and complex social relations, not concrete objects in the world. This inherent difficulty in articulating an appropriate domain of objects of study leads to a sense of methodological insecurity in social psychology. One resolution has been to try to put social psychology theory and method on a sound footing by draw on developments in science that might provide ways of analysing the complexity of social interaction. Lewin (1951), inspired by developments in solid-state physics, had suggested that social psychology could articulate social situations and the actions of individuals on the same plane of reality by invoking the idea of a social field in which individuals and social contexts were constitutive sources of power. Although social situations have an ephemeral existence, they can be analysed as a social field and modelled by mapping the social and individual forces in play that constitute the immediate context of social interaction.

Latané developed and formalised these ideas in his work on what he calls the Law of Social Impact. Brown (1986) expresses the logic behind

Latané's (1981) work on social impact by analogy to Newton's articulation of the laws of gravity. Prior to Newton natural scientists had systematically observed the movements of bodies from everyday objects to the planets and were able to make many predictions about their movements. However, there was no unifying theory that explained the enormous variety of movements from an apple falling from a tree to the circulation of the planets around the sun. Physics provided innumerable specific predictions but had no theory that could link these diverse phenomena. Newton's theory of gravitational forces was a dramatic advance because he was able to formulate a law that could predict the mechanics of all observable bodies of any scale in the known universe. This story of the advances brought by theoretical physics as a way of organising and explaining the enormous variety of scientific observations had particular appeal to social psychologists writing in the 1980s because social psychology appeared to be a field with many interesting studies of social behaviour and a variety of explanations but little in the way of unifying theory. In response, Latané proposed that there are social psychological equivalents of the laws of gravitation, which can play the role of integrating and explaining the diverse findings in the psychology of social influence.

Brown (1986) explains some of the results in the Milgram experiment as instances of the proximity/intensity relation. Milgram found a relationship between proximity and obedience in which he observed that the closer to the victim and more intense the feedback from the learner the less obedience. A metaphor for the mechanics of social power is a light bulb shedding light on a target in which both the intensity of the source (the wattage of the light bulb) and the proximity of the source to the target influence the level of illumination. Latané adopts the idea that social situations have psychological reality because of the constitutive nature of the forces exhibited by both the individuals present and aspects of the social setting. For example, in the Milgram experiment, the three people involved, the experimenter, teacher (participant) and the learner are agents that exert influence on one another. Complementing these social agents, the setting influences and constrains the activities and movements of the people involved. Latané invites us to think of the social context as a force field within which the agents emanate forces that psychologically 'push' the other agents present in certain directions by analogy to the level of illumination that a light bulb can give to an object. A person can affect another according to the intensity of the force that they can emanate and their proximity to the other. Social influence, in other words, is a capacity and the impact arising from that capacity depends upon the intensity of the force and the proximity of the target.

Brown represents a different view of scientific social psychology to Milgram. Latané and Brown believe that social psychology should be a branch of the natural sciences combining careful observation of the complex interactions that constitute social life and explaining these data by developing 'covering laws' that can be used to predict social behaviour. Milgram's approach is different. He does not see social psychology as such a distinct scientific discipline but explicitly draws on social and political theory when framing his research questions. His commitment to science does not come from the search for general laws of social behaviour but from a belief in the value of empirical research to test the psychological assumptions of social and political theory. Milgram connects social psychology to the other social sciences while claiming a specific contribution through the focus on the individual and the use of scientific methods. However, Brown's interpretation is helpful because it highlights that Milgram thinks of power or social influence as a capacity by analogy to physical forces. Although Milgram developed his ideas in the context of broader intellectual debates, in his experiment he treats social influence as a capacity of the authority with measurable effects. I will return to this question of Milgram's assumption about the nature of power in later chapters.

## Recent interpretations of the obedience experiments

Milgram's obedience to authority experiments assure him of a place in the history of social psychology and, as documented in Blass's biography and illustrated by an article in the *New York Times* on the 1st July 2008, his work retains popular appeal and interest. However, the settlement over the meaning of Milgram's work, putting it in the context of the social psychology of social influence, following the influence of Asch and influencing in turn the work of Philip Zimbardo, appears to offer strong support to Arendt's thesis of the banality of evil. Haslam and Reicher (2007) bring this settlement concerning Milgram into question and offer a welcome analysis of experimental research on social influence from the 1960s going back to the social, political and moral debates that originally motivated Asch, Milgram and Zimbardo (see also Reicher and Haslam, 2006).

Haslam and Reicher (2007) suggest that the empirical studies of social psychologists give strong support to the thesis of the banality of evil originally articulated in Arendt's reflections on the Eichmann trial. They argue that the banality of evil thesis has attained the status of consensus within academic discussion in philosophy, history and social psychology and has transcended academic discussion to become part of public imagination. Haslam and Reicher quote Lozowick's claim that the concept of the banality of evil 'has become a permanent feature of Western consciousness, a staple of modern culture' (Haslam and Reicher, 2007, p. 615). Although Milgram had made his request for funds for the obedience experiments after Eichmann's arrest, he did not refer to the Holocaust and Eichmann in the proposal, focusing instead on the example of the army as a context in which people would obey orders without question and wondering how obedient people would be in a less authoritarian context (Blass, 2004). However, as Haslam and Reicher point out, by the time Milgram came to write his first paper in 1963 and even more by the time he wrote his book in 1974, he had come to accept Arendt's analysis of Eichmann as illustrating the banality of evil. Haslam and Reicher suggest that the pairing of social philosophy and empirical social psychology was a powerful combination that established the banality of evil as an accomplished fact in both academic and public imagination.

Haslam and Reicher question the consensus over the banality of evil. They draw on Cesarani's (2004) criticism that Arendt had only attended the first few days of Eichmann's trial in which she heard his defence that he was not personally responsible but was a normal person and a bureaucrat caught up in the administrative system. Haslam and Reicher (2007) reflect on the ways in which the historical record raises doubts about Arendt's analysis of Eichmann:

> First, he was comfortable with Nazi anti-Semitism and found the general ideology of the party congenial. Second, his views were *transformed* in the context of his *increasing identification* with the Nazi movement ... Third, he did not simply follow orders. Rather he pioneered creative, new methods of deportation ... Fourth, Eichmann was well aware of what he was doing and was constantly confronted with the realities of the deaths he caused. Fifth, he was equally aware that others considered his acts to be wrong, but even after the war he

displayed neither remorse nor repentance (Haslam and Reicher, 2007, p. 617).

These ideas challenge the concept of the banality of evil because they demonstrate the purpose, motivation and strategy required for Eichmann to play his role in the Holocaust in contrast to the idea that he was an ordinary man just doing his job. The examples also speak to a complex process of increasing commitment and identification with the Nazi regime and its purposes. Eichmann's contributions to the Holocaust cannot be understood as a mindless decision (as we can rationalise the conduct of people in the Milgram experiment) but as an active enrolment in an evil that was anything but banal. Arendt certainly did not suggest that the evil of the Holocaust was banal, but the suggestion in her argument that Eichmann was banal misses the various ways in which he committed himself to the Nazi cause.

If Arendt's ideas about the banality of evil are problematic as an interpretation of the historical record, this perhaps raises equally difficult challenges to Milgram's explanation of his findings. Here Haslam and Reicher point to some of the questions raised in this book, for example, Milgram's lack of analysis of disobedience and his relative neglect of the evident moral struggles and tactics of his participants. As we have seen, the material from Milgram's own experiments brings into doubt his idea that obedience was the result of participants removing themselves from agency and moral considerations and acting in the agentic state. As Haslam and Reicher argue, if the obedient participants in the Milgram experiment can be interpreted as tactical and engaged, even at the same time that they were obedient to authority, then this leads to the opposite conclusion to Arendt's and Milgram's invocation of the banality of evil.

Haslam and Reicher (2007) offer an alternative analysis of the dynamic process involved in social influence, which goes beyond the polarity in Milgram's work between the autonomous individual and the agentic state. They suggest three dynamics are involved in the relationship between individuals and groups that lead to social influence. First, in contrast to Milgram's claim that personality does not discriminate the obedient from the disobedient, they suggest that there is a more subtle psychology in play in social influence arising from the attractions of identifying with authority or with dominant social groups. Identification potentially emerges from the synergy between the ideology of the group and the preferences and beliefs of the individual. Alternatively, the potential value that member-ship of the group gives to the individual as in the opportunities for career development can bind the individual to the group. The proposal is that social identity develops dynamically as the individual participates and grows into the group and is not an essential quality of individuals expressed or articulated through group membership. The second dynamic arises from the way that group membership transforms the individual's identity:

> Eichmann, in common with many other Nazis, started off with authoritarian leanings but was emboldened through his involvement in the part to embrace and promote ever more extreme ideology and practice that took anti-Semitism to new and ever more abhorrent depths (Haslam and Reicher, 2007, p. 620).

The third dynamic of social influence arises when authoritarianism spreads through social groups, institutions or broader society enrolling individuals in hierarchies, groups and institutions. Haslam and Reicher suggest that the history of the emergence and domination of the German people by the Nazi regime arose through the dispersal of authority through dynamic social influence. Increasing numbers of individuals were enrolled through identification and the transformation of identity, which spread through broader society undermining and eroding alternatives until citizenship and the operation of law fell under almost complete political control.

Haslam and Reicher's analysis raises important challenges to the text-book interpretation of Milgram's obedience experiments. First, they reassert the importance of understanding the role of individuals in social influence against the idea that people are only obedient when they give up on their agency. Second, these ideas demonstrate that Milgram had an interactive but not dynamic view of the relationship between individuals and author-ity and did not take account of the way that enrolment in relations of power changes people. Third, it challenges Milgram's ideas about the way that an individual psychological process of obedience to authority can be transformed into a broader social and political process, going beyond the assumption that there would be mass obedience to authority.

Haslam and Reicher's arguments also imply that thinking about research in social influence, in particular Milgram's obedience experiments requires us to revisit the social and historical context in which Milgram's ideas and experiments were carried out and that we link this analysis to debates in social, moral and political theory. However, it is important to remember

that Haslam and Reicher focus their critique on the textbook representation of Milgram's work and on its role in the social representation of
the banality of evil. As we will see in later chapters, Milgram's writings
provide a more complex and subtle treatment of issues related to power,
the Holocaust and the human condition.

## Conclusions

Milgram's obedience experiments have had a mixed reception in psychology. On the one hand there is a recognition of the importance of the work
but this is tempered by real concerns about the ethics of his procedure,
doubts about the meaning of the results and particularly an almost disre-
gard of Milgram's attempts to explain his results. The criticism that Milgram
has received may seem to be extreme, maybe missing the main point that
his experiments demand our attention, provoke us to think and raise
important questions about power and subjectivity. However, Milgram
claimed to be conducting scientific research and this level of critical attention by peers is essential to scientific endeavour. Milgram recognised this
and fully committed himself to the discussion and debate of his research.
However, the sustained nature and scope of the criticisms leave us with a
paradox since interest in Milgram's research remains undiminished. He is
a mainstay of social psychology textbooks and is still probably the most
talked about example of social psychological research on the media and
among the public (Blass, 2004).

An article in the September 2008 edition of *The Psychologist* the professional publication of the British Psychological Society, reports empirical
research on obedience inspired by Milgram 45 years after the original experiments! The article reports that Jerry Burger, a social psychologist at Santa
Clara University in California is conducting replications of Milgram's original procedure and focusing on the important question of why the moment
of the delivery of 150 volts appears to be a pivotal point beyond which it
is difficult to disobey. This means that obedience experiments could be
ethical if participants were not required to go beyond 150 volts because
we can assume that those who are obedient at this level will continue to
be obedient. Burger suggests that with this modification social psychologists can proceed to conduct experimental research on obedience to authority! Dominic Parker at Ohio State University also supports the importance

of 150 volts in the obedience experiments based on a meta analysis of Milgram's results. The article reflects on recent atrocities by US troops in Iraq have brought Milgram's experiment back onto the public agenda but it also might give an impetus to further psychological studies.

How can we account for the paradox that Milgram's experiments although they are fascinating and important, appear to be impure science, tainted by the scale and importance of the criticisms they have received from the psychology community? I think that this must be because what is interesting about Milgram's experiment and his findings is not the contribution that they make to advance the science of social influence but because of their role as theatre addressed to central concerns about the human condition. In the following chapters of this book, I will explore these meanings of the Milgram experiments by examining the sociological, political and moral dimensions of Milgram's obedience experiments before discussing the other research he conducted in social psychology and the contemporary relevance of his work.

# 4 Power, Domination and the Sociology of the Holocaust

We have seen that Milgram was a talented although controversial experimenter and that he combined this with an eclectic engagement with writers across the social sciences. Milgram was attracted to the interdisciplinary context of the Institute of Social Relations where he could develop his knowledge and skills in psychology while retaining his interest in sociology and political theory. Milgram was generous in his acknowledgement of writers in social theory and sociology, however, he never explicitly wrote about writers such as Adorno, Fromm and Arendt, referring to them in passing rather than developing an account of the sociological context and implications of his work. Milgram was an intellectual optimist and a maverick; he drew on a diversity of sources and brought them together in the design of his empirical studies without worrying too much about the details and inconsistencies between these different theories. Partly I think he wanted to let his results talk for him on these issues and partly he was focused on developing his psychological explanations of the findings. In this chapter, I will explore the sociological background and implications of Milgram's research by examining the influence of Weber, Fromm and critical social theory on his work on obedience. I will then focus on the insights into Milgram's work that emerges from a reading of Bauman's (1989) sociological analysis of the Holocaust.

## Weber

In *Obedience to Authority* Milgram acknowledges Weber as one of the sociologists who established the *Zeitgeist* for social science during his formative years as a graduate student and academic. Weber's ideas about social science methods and his theory of power as legitimate authority influenced Milgram's thinking and fed into his experiments on obedience and his broader commitments as a social psychologist.

Based on his comparative studies and analysis of individuals' experience Weber concluded that modern societies exhibit two characteristic tendencies: individualisation and rationalisation. Individualisation reflects the growing autonomy and freedom of individuals in modern society and rationalisation refers to the way that societies are increasingly organised through the development and spread of social institutions. These themes combined in Weber's work as he sought to characterise the operations of social institutions and the actions of individuals as forms of rationality.

## Weber on method and explanation

During the nineteenth century, as sociology and psychology emerged as separate and identifiable academic disciplines, science and technology were forces that were having a dramatic effect on society. Science appeared to some to be the quintessence of modernity because it was rational, post-traditional, productive and effective. Systematic observation, classification, the experimental method and scientific reasoning were valued, as they still are, as a way of manipulating and explaining the world. Science was changing the place of humans in the order of things giving them control over the physical environment and bending the natural world to their purposes. As the social sciences developed, the idea that the methods and reasoning of science could be applied to the study of society and people was attractive. Perhaps, just as the natural world had been tamed we could also bring order to society and to the lives of people through science. Society could be shaped through social engineering and people enabled to lead better lives through a greater understanding of their own psychology.

Others contested the idea that social groups and individuals could be treated as objects of study in the same way as chemicals and physical forces. They argued that human beings were inherently different to nature and that social scientific methods should reflect this. Unlike molecules or physical processes, human beings have intentions, understanding and act with purpose. The social environment, unlike the mechanical universe of the physical world, is a meaningful social and cultural context. Understanding society and people therefore requires methods that recognised that human beings are self-interpreting agents. Weber was on the side of the argument that different methods were appropriate to study the natural world and the human world. He gave special epistemological status to human beings and treated the individual as the basic unit of empirical study and analysis for social science. If human beings were at the centre of social inquiry, then, Weber argued that social science methods should include an analysis of the subjective experience of individuals and their interpretation of their social environment. Weber did not think that the analysis of individual's beliefs and intentions was all that was required for social analysis but that it should be combined with comparative historical and cultural analysis of society. He advocated looking at societies over different times, and comparing societies from across the world to establish the different forms that social structures and relations could take. Weber sought to combine these two very different approaches to research methods to integrate an analysis of human experience and the comparative analysis of societies.

Weber suggested that social science, through the adoption of a variety of methods would be able to combine explanation with understanding (*Verstehen*). The appropriate method is to empathise with the actor, to see the world through their eyes and engage with them in a way that brings out their reflections on their own conduct and their understanding of the meaning and social context of their actions. The critical assumption of this approach is that agency makes a difference to the choices that individuals make. Milgram follows these principles by putting individuals in a situation in which they had to make a choice that was meaningful to them and would reveal their beliefs about, orientation towards and actions in the face of authority. In addition, he both observed their behaviour and noted their comments during the experiment and their reflections in post-experimental interviews to explore their motivations and understandings.

Milgram also follows Weber in giving special status to the individual. His experiment is a role play between individuals playing out different roles which gives us evidence about the impact of authority as revealed in the interaction between two individuals, one representing institutional power and the other private individuals.

Milgram's reply to Baumrind reflects a sociological influence in his defence that the assumption behind his procedure was that people's actions could make a difference to the world. Milgram is a strong believer in the value of human agency and the capacity of human beings to make choices that shape the social world even when individuals chose to obey authority. Milgram regards broader historical processes as resulting from the actions of individuals impinging on others to create the social world rather than in the idea that individuals are the pawns of social forces that determine their actions.

In contrast to Weber's methodological individualism, Durkheim argued that it is a useful fiction for social scientific research to treat collectives such as families, informal social groups, the public or the nation as if they were agents with thoughts, feelings and perceptions, as having a 'group mind'. Weber does not deny that there are groups and collectives in society but regards these as emerging from the actions of individuals. Le Bon (1999) analysed the crowd as if it were an organism with emotions and cognitions and that social influence worked at the level of the 'social body'. In contrast, Milgram isolates the individual in his laboratory and attempts to reproduce social forces in his experimental context and design.

## Weber on power

Of greater importance is the influence of Weber's distinction between power and domination. He defined power as the capacity of an individual, social group or institution to achieve their aims even in the face of opposition or resistance. For example, the power held by the sovereign in pre-modern society could be exerted on subjects irrespective of their consent or agreement. Weber contrasts this with the way that social influence works in modern societies as domination by legitimate authority. He defines domination as the probability that particular individuals or social groups (Weber, 1968, p. 212) will obey commands. Milgram examined legitimate authority in his obedience experiments through a procedure designed to measure the probability of obedience to commands in different social conditions. Another important feature of domination, which contrasted with power was that domination was widely dispersed across society whereas power tends to be centralised or at the apex of a hierarchy. Weber analysed the operation of dominance in a wide variety of social relationships in different settings to illustrate how modern societies were characterised by the spread of power across a network of social groups and social institutions.

Weber suggested that social influence in the form of domination had certain features. First, domination involves obedience in the form of compliance, such that individuals are not coerced or forced to obey but volunteer or are compliant with authority (Weber, 1968). Milgram went to great lengths to engage participants as volunteers. They actively responded to an advert, the arrangement for them to participate was made over the 'phone at a time of their convenience, they made their own way to the university and were treated as volunteer participants in a psychology experiment. Even when participants found themselves in the uncomfortable circumstances of the experiment itself they were free to leave at any time; certainly no attempt would have been made to stop them leaving and the participants that did disobey indicate that the experiment would stop as soon as they stopped obeying.

Second, Weber also suggests that in relations of domination those who obey do so because they have, or believe that they have an interest in doing so. Some of the comments made by participants in Milgram's experiments indicate that they volunteered to act as participants because they supported the university and believed that it was their civic duty to help the development of public knowledge.

The third feature of legitimate authority according to Weber is the belief in the legitimacy of the authority issuing the commands. Milgram found reduced obedience when he moved the experiment to a non-university setting and when commands were issued by a fellow participant rather than the experimenter there was almost total disobedience. The interviews with participants and the letters they sent Milgram, indicated that they held him and the university in high esteem and that they treated the experimenter as a legitimate authority, entitled to give commands in an experimental context.

Finally, Weber argued that obedience to legitimate authority is typically part of a long-term relationship of domination. This was what Milgram was aiming to demonstrate in his experiments as he argues that for people to behave in the way they did in his experiments was evidence of a widespread conformity and acquiescence amongst the American public. His argument was that the institutions of liberal democracy produced individuals who were used to taking the role of obedient subjects in response to commands from legitimate authorities. In other words, the conduct of the participants in his experiment was only explicable as the result of the way that social dominance had become a structural aspect of liberal democracy. The Milgram experiment works because it taps into long-held beliefs and actions on the part of the participants such that American citizens were participants in their own subordination to authority. Weber documents how different patterns of conformity can arise through habit, custom, convention and discipline. As we have seen, an analysis of the comments and concerns of Milgram's participants reveals that they approach the experiment as embedded in different orders of legitimacy ranging from conventions of politeness and deference to fear of sanctions and the idea that behind the operation of legitimate power stands the power to sanction and punish.

## Authority

> ... modern systems of domination will claim legitimacy through their own rules and legal practices. The right of authorities to issue commands is based on a belief in the formal correctness and validity of the rules (Joseph, 2003, p. 101).

The experimenter in the obedience experiments was accepted by participants and able to command them because they perceived him as a legitimate authority. Weber also influenced Milgram in his analysis of the different forms that authority can take. Weber argues that there are three main types of legitimate authority: traditional, charismatic and rational/legal. Traditional authority refers to authority vested in individuals or social groups based on age-old customs and practices, which precludes challenges to authority and preserves the traditional social order. Charismatic authority or hero worship is obedience to a personality or cult leader. This kind of leadership can break through established traditions and is a powerful force for change but usually does not allow individuals to challenge the authority figure. The third ideal type of authority and the one that is typical of modern systems of domination is rational or legal authority. Authority is accepted when it is embedded in legal structures that confer the right on an appropriately qualified authority to issue orders. When people obey what they see to be a rational command they do so because they believe that it is legitimate. This contrasts with the idea that they follow orders blindly as part of a ritual or tradition or because they are in thrall to a charismatic leader. Rational or legal authority affords the opportunity to individuals to challenge or appeal against the authority. I think this explains both the initial acquiescence of the participants in Milgram's study and that disobedience occurred because as the experiment unfolded some participants defined the harm to the learner as something that could not be justified morally or legally. The administration of a university and the role of a professor are both grounded in law, in statute, in university rules and regulations. Participants in Milgram's experiment assumed that all this was in place behind the experimenter and legitimated the issuing of orders and justified their obedience at the beginning of the experiment.

Weber argues that the critical difference between traditional or charismatic authority on the one hand and rational or legal forms of authority is that those who are subject to its commands can challenge the latter. The participants who disobeyed and the protests and questions of those who obeyed indicate that the participants in the Milgram experiment believed that they were confronting an authority that was legitimised legally and rationally. Another aspect of modern forms of authority is that they work at a distance and do not depend upon personal relationship between the authority and the subject. The participants in Milgram's experiments would certainly have been used to the idea of obeying authorities and they would be aware of how this relationship of domination and consent is embedded in broader bureaucratic and legal arrangements. However, they would also have been aware that in the background of legitimate authority sits the organisational culture of modernity, the means of violence and the ability to apply sanctions. In this context, their hesitancy in resisting authority is understandable as much as their inclination to obey.

Milgram confronted his participants with a moral dilemma, but he did so by designing an experiment that created a context that gave mixed messages about the relations of domination. Several features of the experimental context cued the participants into thinking that they were in the context of a relationship of domination through discipline. The institutional setting, the role of the experimenter in taking control and issuing instructions, the ritual and rule bound procedure of the laboratory would all have cued participants to expect instructions. Under these circumstances, participants act as disciplined subjects and follow the commands of authority. Then, as the experiment unfolds, the participants slowly realised that they were being asked to make a choice that had consequences for the learner and that to disobey would require them to challenge the legitimacy of the authority of the experimenter.

## Were the obedience studies experiments?

The links between Weber and Milgram's experiment that I discuss here raise important methodological questions. Milgram's view was that his experiments were a theoretically neutral test of the psychological assumptions of moral, social and political theory. However, it is evident from the links between his design and the social theory of Weber, that Milgram's experiment was not a neutral mechanism for discovering the truth of the matter of obedience but an operationalisation of Weber's social and political theory of the modern state. Key features of his construction of the individual as subject and legitimate authority, the operation of dominance through command, the distinction between discipline and choice and the questions raised by participants about the legality and legitimacy of the experiments all reflect Weber's theoretical discussion of the relationship of domination between the state and individuals. Milgram's experiment is a performative demonstration of some of the ideas that he had been reading mixed with his concerns about the passivity of citizens in post-war USA and his reflection on the Holocaust.

## Fromm

Milgram cites Erich Fromm's book *Escape from Freedom* as a strong influence on his work on obedience to authority. Fromm begins his book with a discussion of the concept of 'freedom', which he places at the centre of the human condition. He reflects on the erosion of hard won human rights and freedoms in emerging totalitarian regimes in the early years of the twentieth century:

> For the essence of these new systems, which effectively took control of man's entire social and personal life, was the submission of all but a handful of men to an authority over which they had no control (Fromm, 1941, p. 4).

Fromm, like Milgram later, was particularly concerned with the rise of Nazi Germany out of liberal democracy. He considers and dismisses a variety of explanations for the rise of fascism in Germany: the madness of Germany's leaders, the lack of maturity of German democracy, political cunning and intrigue. Instead, Fromm suggests that domination partly resulted from the inability of individuals to cope, psychologically, with the freedoms granted to the citizen of modern liberal democratic society. Fromm took these ideas from Weber and suggested that they would affect individuals' psychology in characteristic ways:

> We have been compelled to recognize that millions in Germany were as eager to surrender their freedom as their fathers were to fight for it;

that instead of wanting freedom, they sought for ways of escape from it (Fromm, 1941, p. 4).

Fromm emphasised that although Nazi Germany offered a particularly extreme formulation of the escape from freedom, the problem was just as relevant in liberal democracies. He quotes John Dewey in a way that, I think, made a big impression on Stanley Milgram:

> The serious threat to our democracy is not the existence of foreign totalitarian states. It is the existence within our own personal attitudes and within our own institutions of conditions which have given a victory to external authority, discipline and uniformity and dependence upon The Leader in foreign countries. The battlefield is also accordingly here – within ourselves and our institutions (Dewey, 1939, cited in Fromm, 1941, p. 5).

This combination of concerns about Nazi Germany and conformity in the USA was a feature of Milgram's work that he derived from Fromm. Fromm aims to understand the reasons why humans might give up on striving for freedom under certain social conditions and he proposes that freedom might create an unbearable psychological burden. This idea resonates with Milgram's explanation of the way that obedience results from submission grounded in our biological heritage and reactions to authority. Fromm suggests that widespread submission in modern societies includes obedience to authority, the internalisation of authority in conscience and conformity to public opinion. He argues that social problems such as the rise of conformity and obedience to authority are at least in part psychological phenomena resulting from an evolutionary hangover and which are instinctive and emotional rather than rational. In this, Fromm acknowledges his debt to Freud who established the importance of irrational and unconscious psychological forces. However, Fromm argues against Freud's assumption that human nature is derived from our biology and that society influences human character by suppression and redirection of instinctual drives. The implication is that human nature is primarily biologically determined and can only be channelled and influenced but not formed by social contexts and forces. In contrast, Fromm argues for a focus on the relationship between individuals and the social world in different societies at different times and that human nature is a product of social relations and interactions:

> Although there are certain needs, such as hunger, thirst, sex, which are common to man, those drives that make the differences in men's characters, like love and hatred, the lust for power and the yearning for submission...are all products of the social process (Fromm, 1941, p. 12).

Fromm argues that in modern societies, individuals have the opportunity to grasp 'positive freedom' by embracing the opportunities of self-expression through work and family life. The alternative is to give up on freedom, to look for ways of escaping its burdens. Fromm suggested three examples of escape from freedom: authoritarianism, destructiveness and conformity. In authoritarianism, individuals give up on the potential for expressing their individuality and embrace powerful social collectives as a means of overcoming feelings of aloneness and powerlessness. In totalitarian regimes, this is the common experience, but even in liberal democracies, this tendency shows itself in the immersion of the individual in public opinion:

> Instead of overt authority, 'anonymous' authority reigns. It is disguised as common sense, science, psychic heath, normality, public opinion. It does not demand anything except the self-evident. It seems to use no pressure but only mild persuasion (Fromm, 1941).

What results is a loss of identity:

> ...the individual ceases to be himself; he adopts entirely the kind of personality offered to him by cultural patterns; and he therefore becomes exactly as all others are and as they expect him to be. The discrepancy between 'I' and the world disappears and with it the conscious fear of aloneness and powerlessness (Fromm, 1941).

Fromm applied these ideas to an analysis of the popular politics of Nazism in which individuals could escape the burdens of freedom, isolation and anxiety by embracing a powerful social movement linked to national identity. He then applied the analysis to modern America, acknowledging that the liberal democracy in the USA had granted individuals freedom from constraints. However, Fromm nevertheless argued that this might not amount to positive freedom but an illusion of freedom:

> By conforming with the expectations of others, by not being different, these doubts about one's own identity are silenced and a certain security is gained. However, the price is high. Giving up spontaneity and individuality thwarts life...positive freedom consists in the spontaneous activity of the total, integrated personality (Fromm, 1941).

These ideas clearly influenced Milgram in the design of his obedience experiments. His view of his participants was that they faced the challenge of freedom and he set a test of their character that would demonstrate whether they could express their individuality in positive freedom or would conform to discipline. In Fromm's terms, Milgram's experiment demonstrates that ordinary people in early 1960s America were escaping from freedom by siding with authority and seeking to conform. Milgram, like Fromm, was convinced that if US citizens were inclined to escape from freedom then they were vulnerable to the influence of authoritarian regimes, which led him to believe that there was an inherent danger that an authoritarian regime might appeal to the American people. These ideas had a particular resonance in the context of post-war USA in which the Cold War provided an external threat from totalitarian regimes accompanied by the risks that arose from the internal social changes that potentially caused disruption and personal alienation. I will return to these issues in the next chapter when I explore the political dimensions of Milgram's work.

## Critical social theory in the USA

Fromm developed his ideas in sympathy with a group of academics called the Frankfurt School. The critical agenda set by the Frankfurt School also had a strong influence on Milgram. They established that a critical social analysis of western liberal democracy would have three main themes: the criticism of contemporary culture, authoritarianism, and bureaucratisation (Held, 1980, p. 39). These critical theorists shifted the focus away from the question of whether capitalism was a viable alternative to socialism towards the question of whether the freedom offered by the new liberal democracies was a positive freedom realised in the everyday lives of its citizens. This marked an important shift: instead of comparisons between different societies (e.g. between the US and the Soviet Union), critical attention shifted to internal, domestic US society and politics. New questions emerged as to whether this new society, a liberal democracy that offered opportunity and protection to its citizens through the potential for their personal development as citizen consumers, delivered on its promise of personal freedom in an open society (Jamison and Eyerman, 1994).

Jamison and Eyerman neatly sum up the image of mainstream US culture in the writings of Riesman, Adorno, Fromm, Arendt, Mills and others:

> The society that emerged out of the Second World War was given many names, as it evoked images of conformity, loneliness, homogenization, standardization, and mediocrity. Individuals had become faceless figures in grey flannel suites, working in anonymous organizations and living in ... little boxes (Jamison and Eyerman, 1994, p. 34).

The critique of post-war liberal democracy had a strong influence on Milgram. These radical thinkers adapted their critical analysis of totalitarian society in Germany and Russia onto the new consumer society emerging in post-Second World War America. Alienation, which once meant lack of power in relation to production, was re-interpreted as a personal alienation in a meaningless existence. Totalitarian oppression was translated into social conformity in a consumer society. The iron cage of rationality was translated into the binding power of the rhythms of the workplace and the habits of consumer society. Ideology was no longer understood as a dominant set of beliefs but a more subtle enrolment of individuals into social and political processes backed by the persuasive rhetoric of popular culture. The threat to democracy came from the dispersal and fragmentation of the public and their diversion by consumer culture rather than from oppression so that the public were less likely to act collectively to oppose state and commercial power. The suburb, the emblem of the new prosperity and opportunity was reinterpreted as the symbol of a new set of social problems that are recognisable to us today: lack of social cohesion, anti-social behaviour, social isolation and the sustainability of the city.

The radical intellectuals that Milgram clearly admired were operating in a period of conformity, political consensus and stability and they kept alive the flame of radicalism and a politically committed social science (Jamison and Eyerman, 1994). All of these ideas made a strong impression on Stanley Milgram. As a social psychologist, he used the tools at his disposal (experimental method and psychological explanation) to contribute to the analysis of the travails of liberal democracy by staging a dramatic representation of the vulnerability of individuals in the face of authority.

## Talcott Parsons and structural functionalism

Talcott Parsons was the head of the institute of social relations and Milgram attended his lectures when he was a graduate student. Parsons took key ideas from Weber and Durkheim and attempted to integrate them.

Weber's ideas about power and authority had a direct influence on Milgram, as did Durkheim's view of society as a functional system and the individual as a subsystem of society. Talcott Parsons suggests that a combination of conformity and socialisation make social cohesion possible given the complexity and diversity of modern society (Joseph, 2003, p. 83). Through socialisation, individuals internalise a moral order based on common values that forms the basis of social order. Functionalist analysis asks which actions contribute to social stability and whether this results from shared values or normative rules (Joseph, 2003, p. 83). Functionalism analyses individual's actions and patterns of actions across individuals to see whether they contribute to or detract from social cohesion.

Parsons main concern was to explain how complex, large scale, modern societies are ordered. The relative freedoms of modern life and the differentiation of social roles and social groups mean that there is a differentiation between the way that people live and social institutions. Parsons argued that processes of adaptation, goal attainment, integration and latency linked social interaction and structure. In relation to the Milgram experiment, the influence of the setting of the university illustrates the way that the physical environment partly structures social interaction. In Goal attainment, participants are mobilised by the potential to align their goals those of the social system. In the Milgram experiment, the experimenter took the authority to set the goals of the experimental context and procedure and assigned roles to the participants. Integration refers to the way in which culture maintains social cohesion or solidarity and subsystems are coordinated. The method of integration in the Milgram experiment is command and obedience. Latency, in Parson's theory refers to the patterns of social behaviour through which adaptation, goal attainment and integration are maintained and consolidated. The interaction in the Milgram experiment illustrates the operation of power in the way that the experimenter establishes the goals and organises the activity of the participants. Obedience links the individual to the social system through the performance of social roles expressing the internalisation of social norms:

> Parsons is therefore concerned with the psychological aspect of social life in terms of the dispositions of social agents, their internalization of social norms and their performance of a role (Joseph, 2003, p. 87).

All these elements are in play in the Milgram experiments in which the disposition to obey authority and value individual autonomy are put into conflict, the individuals demonstrate that they have internalised these social norms and value them, and that they have been socialised to play out social roles.

One criticism of Parsons' work is that he is so focused on the systematic integration of society, culture and subjectivity that he underestimates the level of conflict in society. Conflicts of interest, divergent views and different ways of living are surely as much a part of modern liberal democracies as conformity and obedience. This preference for the view of society as a coherent system had a strong influence on Milgram. As we have seen, he focused mainly on obedience and did not pay enough attention to disobedience and the attempts by his participants to challenge and bring authority to account.

## The sociology of the Holocaust

The Holocaust is a constant reference point in Milgram's work and in his life (Blass, 2004). However, there have been disputes in the psychological literature about whether or what the Milgram experiment tells us about the Holocaust and he appeared to be ambivalent about the connection and at times was at pains to point out that this was not his main concern. Commenting on the way that Gordon

Allport referred to his work as 'The Eichmann experiment' Milgram wrote:

> The 'Eichmann experiment', is, perhaps, an apt term, but it should not lead us to mistake the import of this investigation. To focus only on the Nazis, however despicable their deeds and to view only highly publicised atrocities as being relevant to these studies is to miss the point entirely. For the studies are principally concerned with the ordinary and routine destruction carried out by everyday people following orders (Milgram, 1974, p. 178).

In this quote, it is apparent that Milgram's main concerns were with the state of conformity in his own society and that the Holocaust stands as an extreme case and a warning. Nevertheless, Milgram mentions the Holocaust many times in his papers and books and the relation of his work to the Holocaust as part of the background to his interests in obedience. However, he does not work through the implications of his findings for understanding the Holocaust, even though that is one of the main arguments that textbooks give for the importance of his work. Fortunately, Zygmunt Bauman, in his book *Modernity and the Holocaust*, makes a serious attempt to answer Milgram's main question: what are the implications of reflection on the Holocaust for contemporary society? Bauman is motivated, as Milgram was, to keep the events of the Holocaust alive and in the memories of those who did not experience them, but also to make the Holocaust a lens through which we can reflect upon the nature of modern society.

Bauman provides us with an excellent way of reflecting on these questions, which I believe will help us to understand Milgram's reflections on the Holocaust. In addition, Bauman offers a sociological interpretation of Milgram's obedience experiments as part of his book *Modernity and the Holocaust*, which follows his discussion of Arendt's work on the Eichmann trial and ideas derived from her work *The Human Condition*.

## Bauman's modernity and the Holocaust

Bauman reflects on how, before working on his book, he thought about the Holocaust as a stereotypical portrayal of 'a horrible crime, visited by the wicked on the innocent' (Bauman, 1989, p. vii). He describes the experience of reading the memoirs of his wife Janine Bauman, a Holocaust survivor, in *Beyond These Walls*:

> I began to think just how much I did not know – or rather, did not think about properly... What happened was far too complicated to be explained in that simple and intellectually comforting way I naively imagined sufficient (Bauman, 1989, pp. vii–viii).

Bauman describes how having read widely from the literature on the Holocaust in history, social science and psychology, he was struck by the relative lack of sociological writing and so he determined to write a book in this area. He outlines the key ideas that emerged from this reading and argues that looking at the details of the events of the Holocaust led him to question his stereotypical understanding in uncomfortable ways. In particular, he came to believe that the Holocaust was not something apart from history but a part of it and that an adequate sociology of modern societies must include an analysis of the Holocaust:

> ... the Holocaust is not simply a Jewish problem, and not an event in Jewish history alone. The Holocaust was born and executed in our modern and rational society, at the high stage of our civilization and at the peak of human cultural achievement and for this reason it is a problem of that society, civilization and culture (Bauman, 1989, p. x).

Like Arendt before him, Bauman is critical of stereotypes of the Holocaust as the expression of evil, combined with the latent anti-Semitism of Germans and made possible because of a particular extreme state of the Third Reich at war. In contrast, the tradition initiated by Arendt and carried forward by Bauman, and of which Milgram is clearly a part, points to the continuities between Germany under the Nazis and other modern states, including the US in the 1950s and contemporary society. Bauman expresses a sentiment that I think Milgram would have wholly subscribed to that there is a danger that:

> The message which the Holocaust contains about the way we live today – about the quality of the institutions on which we rely for our safety, about the validity of the criteria by which we measure the propriety of our own conduct and the pattern of interactions we

accept and consider normal – is silenced, not listened to, and remains undelivered (Bauman, 1989, p. xii).

For Milgram, in the context of 1950s America, just as for Bauman today, the lessons of the Holocaust served as a means of reflection on contemporary society. In the social psychology of social influence, Le Bon had argued that following the crowd was something that emanated from being part of a pre-civilised, primitive collective. Arendt, Milgram and Bauman all argue against the idea that the Holocaust happened when civilisation was swept away. Instead, they insist that the seeds of the Holocaust were diverse and reflect the normal civilised functioning of social institutions and the conduct of ordinary citizens going about their everyday lives.

In the early chapters of his book, Bauman reviews previous writings on the Holocaust in sociology and analyses the features of modern societies that contributed to the Holocaust. These include the breakdown of traditional order, the entrenchment of modern nation-states, the link between racism and genocide, the adoption of social engineering and the important role of science in legitimation. However, how did these features, which are common to modern societies, contribute to the unique conditions that brought about the Holocaust? Bauman suggests that the Holocaust emerged from a particular combination of these features of modernity:

> ... the emancipation of the political state, with its monopoly on the means of violence and its audacious engineering ambitions, from social control – following the step-by-step dismantling of all non-political power resources and institutions of social self-management (Bauman, 1989, p. xiii).

This is an important part of Bauman's argument and leads him to articulate what he takes to be the unique configuration of features of modern societies that led to the Holocaust. He reminds us that in Germany as late as 1941, the full extent of the Holocaust was still unanticipated and that many could or would not believe it as it unfolded. However, Bauman argues that the conditions of possibility for the Holocaust were in place. One implication of this is that people were unaware of the power of the state in modern society and that assumptions that administrative institutions, civil society and the actions of individuals are powerful enough to resist government may be unfounded. An important implication of this analysis of the Holocaust is that liberal democracy appears to involve the potential or the risk of the emergence of a powerful state that might, under particular conditions, act in a systematic and unconstrained way. Bauman quotes a number of scholars who have proposed this view:

> Within certain limits set by political and military power considerations, the modern state may do anything it wishes to those under its control. There is no moral-ethical limit which the state cannot transcend if it wishes to do so, because there is no moral-ethical power higher than the state. In matters of ethics and morality, the situation of the individual in the modern state is in principle roughly equivalent to the situation of the prisoner in Auschwitz (Kren and Rappaport, Cited in Bauman, 1989, p. 86).

One of the implications of Milgram's experiment is that it demonstrates that the moral and ethical resources of ordinary individuals in early 1960s USA were, in important respects, roughly equivalent to individuals in a totalitarian state. The implication is that we should not depend upon individuals to bring the state to account, because of the discipline of obedience and the limited scope for individuals to challenge authority. However, Bauman suggests that we exercise caution in this argument, because while we can find numerous parallels between Nazi Germany and the USA in the 1950s, contemporary western, liberal democracies reflected in the tendency of individuals to obey authority in the Milgram experiments, this is not enough to say that a Holocaust will inevitably arise in such societies. Milgram's findings can be read as the 'first signs' of a process that will inevitably lead to relations of domination being transformed into relations of power and Milgram himself appeared to invite this link. As Bauman neatly expresses it:

> having to choose between conformity and bearing the consequences of disobedience does not necessarily mean living in Auschwitz, and the principles preached and practised by most contemporary states do not suffice to make their citizens into Holocaust victims (Bauman, 1989, p. 87).

According to Bauman, we cannot identify in the way we live now the green shoots of a process that will inevitably lead to another Holocaust. However, the parallels between our own and genocidal societies demonstrate two things that we should be very concerned about. First, that the political ideology and implementation of the mechanisms of genocide are compatible with civilisation and second, that the checks and balances against power that we hope are an integral part of civilised society are limited and under certain conditions will fail us.

Following these ideas of Bauman's, we can now suggest an alternative interpretation of Milgram's findings. The obedience experiments demonstrate graphically that authority and deference are an integral part of the social ordering of liberal democracy and that consequently one of the checks and balances that we believe to be in place, the ability of individuals to assert their rights to challenge and bring authority to account, is open to question. In addition, Milgram demonstrated that people had wrongly predicted that participants in the obedience experiments would resist authority far more than they did. This suggests that there are widespread beliefs, perhaps complacent beliefs, that the institutions of civil society, social groups and individuals will resist any attempt by the state to take unreasonable powers. In addition, I think it is clear from the accounts that Milgram's participants gave of their experience in the experiments that citizens of liberal democracies strongly believed and rely upon the conviction that authority is self-governing and will impose limitations on its own power.

Although many of the participants in the experiments were unable to disobey the experimenter, they were not entirely passive in the face of authority. There were many examples of protest, questioning authority, appealing on behalf of the victim, making sure that the experimenter knew that they were distressed and opposed to what was happening. This speaks to a particular understanding of the way that power worked in the context of the Milgram experiment and gives us clues as to how people understand power to operate in western liberal democracy. Following de Certeau we can say that individuals appear to accept the right of the authority to strategic power (to define the situation and to issue commands) and that they see themselves as having tactical power to challenge, divert and attempt to deal with the consequences of the implementation of authority (de Certeau, 1984).

This allows us to modify Milgram's interpretation of 'disobedience', since he defined this strictly in terms of the outcome of the experiment as participants 'choosing' not to stop the experiment and disobey the experimenter. However, what Milgram demonstrates is not that people are passive victims of authority but that they deploy a range of tactics to deal with the consequences of authority and they deploy these tactics even when they feel unable to affect the outcome. The participants in the Milgram experiment may well have assumed that they were in practice appealing to alternative authorities outside the experimental situation. They also may have reasoned that an external review would judge them to have done their best, and that the experimenter would be held responsible, not them, for the consequences of the experiment on the learner. The experiment isolates the individual as the subject of authority from the broader social context. Milgram designed his experiment as self-contained and controlled. In contrast, the participants saw themselves in a situation that would ultimately be corrected, judged and evaluated as part of a broader system of justice and accountability.

Bauman sees the Holocaust as part of modernity and that it demonstrates the relative powerlessness of individuals in modern society. He then turns his attention to explaining the unique circumstances that turned the potential for mass murder that is part of modernity into a reality. The first argument that Bauman makes is that the Holocaust is not a continuation of previous historical examples of mass murder, genocide and pogrom. The Nazi state used violence as a means of terror and social control to dispose of potential sources of opposition and resistance. However, the Nazi state also made use of systematic and organised administrative and social processes in the pursuit of power, which complemented the direct use of violence. Bauman cites a chilling quote from Sabini and Silver:

> Thorough, comprehensive, exhaustive murder required the replacement of the mob with a bureaucracy, the replacement of shared rage with obedience to authority. The requisite bureaucracy would be effective whether manned by extreme or tepid anti-Semites … it would govern the actions of its members not by arousing passions but by organizing routines (Sabini and Silver, 1980, quoted in Bauman, 1989, p. 90).

This planned, organised activity radically broadened the capability and scope of the Holocaust when compared to previous genocides and pogroms. Sabini and Silver (1980) agree with Milgram's implicit questioning of the applicability of Le Bon's theory of the crowd as an explanation of the Holocaust. However, Milgram's findings take this argument further because obedience to authority in his experiments occurs without the presence of the large-scale bureaucracy of a totalitarian regime. Milgram seems to demonstrate that the potential for complicity with rationalised systems of genocide exists in the propensity of individuals to obey authority and that very little is required in terms of bureaucracy and social control to bring about complicity. His experimental context was, after all, an isolated, controlled, liminal space in a society that was very different from Nazi Germany. However, the point is clear, Milgram's participants were decidedly not part of an angry mob, they had no reason to hate the learner in the experiment and there is no evidence that they felt themselves to be part of a broader system of rigid social control, yet many of them still obeyed authority against their better judgement.

Bauman suggests that these actions of individuals who implemented genocide without hatred and primitive emotional expression as part of a mob tell us something important about the nature of the culture of modernity. Rationalisation in the form of classification, tidiness, standards and order for the sake of order implemented on a large scale is characteristic of modern society. We can discern these trends in modernity in the control and manipulation of nature and the technical application of instrumental, scientific reason. In a morality reflecting Aristotle's conception of actions aimed at making the world a better, more beautiful place, Bauman suggests that behind the bureaucracy and technology of genocide, in modern societies lays an attempt to engineer the social world reflecting an image of a racially and socially pure society. Modern societies developed plumbing and drainage to clean the city and civil engineering focused on human society in an extension of eugenics aimed at producing a thoroughly modern, organised and efficient society.

On this reading the Holocaust arose from a combination of the appropriation of the means of violence by an ideologically obsessed power elite who unhooked themselves from the checks and balances of civilised society and used the technologies of rationalisation characteristic of the modern state to deliver their ideological purposes (Bauman, 1989, p. 94). What Milgram adds to this is how vulnerable people are to such circumstances given their propensity to obey authority and their inability to resist orders and assert their individual rights and power.

## Bureaucracy and terror

Another dimension of modernity that Bauman links to the Holocaust is the division of labour, which leads to the distantiation, and the consequent irrelevance of the moral stance of individuals to the efficient running of bureaucratically organised activities. The division of labour leads to specialisation of action and greater distance between actions and consequence, as individuals become cogs in a hierarchically organised regime. This was critical to the Holocaust because it created a distance between those involved in the organisation of the genocide and the victims and between those planning genocide and those executing it. The tendency of bureaucratic systems to dehumanise the people who are dealt with by their processes contributed to this rationalisation as people become numbers and were treated as objectified entities rather than human beings.

Milgram was aware of these arguments and this is why he developed the manipulation of proximity in his experiments and demonstrated that the further the victim was from the teacher the more obedience to authority ensued. However, Milgram also reports that when there is greater distance between the experimenter and the teacher then disobedience reduces. This is a consistent finding in Milgram's research, which Bauman leaves out of his otherwise reasonable account of Milgram's experiments. Bauman claims that Milgram's experiments demonstrate that obedience is inversely related to social distance confirming that the individual who is a functionary in the bureaucratic machinery of genocide is distant both from the ideological origins of the plans (as they are simply a cog in a chain of authority) and from the consequences for the victims of those plans. This explanation of the inverse relationship between social distance and obedience works well for the relationship between the teacher and the learner. In the experiment, the functional division of labour between the teacher and the learner does indeed contribute to the disengagement of the moral judgement of the participants, and the distance between the teacher and learner increases obedience. However, the opposite occurs in relation to the distance between the learner and the teacher because the direct presence of the experimenter, the authority figure, appears to be necessary for obedience to occur. Milgram's participants took every opportunity they could to disobey and any diminution of the presence or unique authority of the experimenter brought about radical reductions in obedience.

This again, I think reflects the difference between the position of Milgram's participants and functionaries in the bureaucratic machinery of Nazi Germany. In Nazi Germany, the distance of individuals from power exacerbated their feelings of lack of personal power whereas Milgram's participants were ready to disobey at the first signs of weakening of the resolve and vigilance of authority. Milgram's participants did not take up the position of functionaries in an extended system of social control playing out the orders of a powerful state. When the gaze of the experimenter was off them, they showed themselves to be citizens of the USA in the early 1960s ready to take responsibility and challenge authority.

## Power, civilisation and violence

Bauman discusses Norbert Elias's argument in *The Civilizing Process* that the removal of violence from everyday life made civilisation possible in modern society. Violence is sequestered or removed from everyday life, concentrated in the police, armed forces and expressed in rituals and sport. Elias argues against the idea that modernity and civilisation are synonymous with the conquering of violence. On the contrary, modern societies contain, manage and use violence. According to Elias, individuals pay a high price for the peace and security that characterises their everyday life. They are subject to constraint if they are violent, have to give up on the means of violence and are highly vulnerable to oppressive state power. This removes the potential for violence that otherwise would be dispersed amongst groups and individuals in society so that if the state were to turn violence against the public they would be defenceless.

This theory provides an alternative explanation of the acquiescence of the public in the Milgram experiments. In the face of direct orders from authority, they played out the social contract in which authority can wield its power over them as the price of their relative freedom and the relative peace of their society. Bauman demonstrates that institutions that potentially protect people failed to do so in Nazi Germany. Evans (2006) describes how institutions that might have been the focus of opposition to the Nazi regime were systematically undermined and co-opted. Science, instead of offering a position of neutrality or critique served the Nazi regime. The churches too were relatively silent in the face of the growing atrocity of the Nazi regime. Alternative sources of power were eradicated and the broader civic culture was denuded reducing sources of criticism and alternative social norms. As we have seen, Milgram's participants were relying on the existence of plural forms of authority to bring the experimenter potentially to account.

All this reflected Milgram's concerns about the way that academia failed to react strongly to attempts by security forces and the state to put pressure on universities to dismiss academics with a history of sympathy or engagement with radical politics during the Cold War. The relative passivity of university administrators and the lack of protest from academics and students demonstrated that universities were no longer the site of critique and opposition to excessive power from the state. Milgram's experiment was a morality play, signifying the capacity of universities and science to act in the oppression of citizens and indicating that the culture of conformity had permeated even those institutions that one might hope would carry the flame of resistance.

These issues reflect the way that the Nazi regime solicited the co-operation of the institutions of civil society and its victims. This issue and the discussions of it in Arendt's work resonate with Milgram's concern:

> The Jewish population was virtually exempt (in Germany gradually; in the conquered territories abruptly) from the jurisdiction of normal administrative authorities, and thrust fully and without qualification into the hands of their co-religious leaders, who in turn received their orders from, and reported to, a German institution similarly exempt from the 'normal' power structure (Bauman, 1989, p. 121).

Bauman then reconsiders Hannah Arendt's controversial and much discussed account of Jewish collusion in oppression. Against the argument for collusion is the strong argument that the Jewish authorities in question felt they had no alternative; it was an enforced compliance. Outside Germany, for example in Poland, Jewish leaders who failed to comply were simply done away with until leaders were found who did. Whether we accept the argument for collusion or for enforced compliance, the resonances with Milgram's experiment are important and help us to understand a number of features of Milgram's design. For example, the participants in Milgram's experiment were isolated and cut off from all normal social contacts and legal powers and representatives. Their only personal contacts during the experiment were the experimenter and the learner, who turned out to be the experimenter's confederate. Consequently, they were on their own faced with an oppressive authority and they had to do business with their oppressor. Milgram was at pains to emphasise that there was no direct coercion of the participants in his experiments. However, he understates how the isolation of the individual from the 'normal' role of authorities and the open and dispersed nature of powers within which a citizen of the USA in the early 1960s would normally have operated influenced their experience and conduct in the experiment.

## The morality of survival

The standard explanation in social psychology textbooks, that Milgram's participants put aside moral concerns, is shared by Milgram himself in his concept of the agentic state in which rational and moral reasoning is abandoned. Some moral philosophers claim that Milgram's experiments demonstrate that moral agency cannot result from human qualities and character but resides in the influence of social situations on human conduct (Doris, 2002; Harman, 1999). In contrast, Bauman argues that as the Holocaust played itself out it locked those involved into a game of death and survival in a context that kept the illusion of choice and potential freedom alive even at the moment of people's demise. These barely imaginable contradictions were a consequence of people's complete powerlessness accompanied by small clues that survival was possible whether through reclassification or by playing a role in the administration of the state or even genocide; a horrific choice to place in front of a human being, yet that was the choice faced by many in the Holocaust. The minor agonies of the participants in the Milgram experiments reflected this as they struggled to keep open the possibility of negotiating with the authority at the same time as executing the orders to electrocute the learner to the point of death. The appeals to the authority by participants and the attempt to address authorities and norms outside the context of the experiment demonstrate how under co-option by a malevolent authority, individuals try at all costs to keep alive the possibility for rationality and freedom even as they succumb to control.

## Conclusions

We have seen that an important way of thinking about Milgram's experiments emerges from sociological analysis of power and domination. Some participants in Milgram's experiments protested to the authority figure and in effect, were appealing to authority to act in a restrained and self-governing way. If we think of this as an interaction between two agents who have enormously different positions in relation to power then we could say that the participants in Milgram's experiment were assuming that authority would be civilised and would listen to their appeals to constrain power. The analogy that comes to mind is that of a subject in front of a monarch or a court appealing for clemency on behalf of another individual. The submissiveness of the participants in Milgram's experiments is a particular act: submission both acknowledges the power of the authority and demands as a subject that the authority acts reasonably. In other words, the participants in Milgram's experiments were acting on particular assumptions about the relative powers of authority and those subject to the commands of authority.

This account also reveals a very important feature of the Milgram experiment: that much of the power in the situation resided in the hands of the authority, both the power to define the situation and to direct people's actions in the situation. In the context of the experiment, there was no alternative authority to which the participants could appeal. Milgram's experiment mirrors the degree to which the state becomes both the ultimate and the sole source of power in totalitarian states and it is one of the things that made the situation an unusual set of circumstances for ordinary American participants. In Milgram's experiments, power was concentrated in the hands of a single individual, combining both the ideational dimensions of power (defining the purpose and meaning of the situation) and the capacity dimensions of power (having the power to command the actions of others).

Yet there is evidence that Milgram's participants tried to sustain the idea that the authority of the experimenter is embedded in broader systems of authority, power, ethics and law. This contrasts with Milgram's assumptions, derived from systems theory and cybernetics, that the system of authority is an authority hierarchy. Power disperses through the institutions and practices of liberal democracies in contrast to its concentration in the Nazi state. People would have reasonably assumed that there were institutional contexts of accountability that the experimenter would be subject to, that they, as individuals were not the only court of judgement that the experimenter would face and that, consequently, although they might be reasonably expected to voice their concerns, even to protest, they were not ultimately responsible. Indeed their protests could reasonably be seen as the kind of actions that might lead to the experimenter being made accountable to other authorities, as when a pupil complains about their treatment by a teacher or a customer about a product they have purchased. Participants in the Milgram experiments expected their complaints to be taken up, not necessarily by the experimenter but by others who will judge their actions and those of the experimenter. Individuals in liberal democracies believe in the broader system of accountability even in the face of specific examples of corrupt or malevolent authority.

# 5 Political Culture, Political Psychology and Social Influence

In the epilogue of *Obedience to Authority*, Milgram reiterates the point that the issue of the power of authority is a central problem of liberal democracy. He acknowledges that voting allows a degree of power to the people but that in liberal democracy, authority is granted to political leaders and social institutions so that there is a constant need to bring authority to account. Milgram grew up in the dynamic and diverse Jewish immigrant community of the Bronx in the 1930s and 1940s, a context which encouraged radical politics and action (Blass, 2004). Blass cites an example in which Milgram recalls the community occupying the streets in order to force the local authority to make them safer. What intrigued Milgram was whether there were limits to the capacity of individuals to challenge authority in the modern world as their ties to tradition and community weakened. In addition, Milgram's personal circumstances as the child of immigrant parents who struggled financially promoted reflection on the privations that individuals can suffer even in the promised land of America. Blass (2004) documents that Milgram's family suffered many hardships during his childhood and teenage years and that Milgram himself had to work hard to fund his university education since he could not rely on financial support from his family. In other words, Milgram, like many young people of his age and background had a heightened political awareness, a commitment to liberal politics and a concern with the relative powerlessness of individuals.

Milgram's choice of a first degree in political science reflected his interest in politics and exposed him to debates on the nature of democracy. In *Obedience to Authority,* he refers to Hobbes and to de Tocqueville's *Democracy in America*, which contrasts the form of democracy, developing in the USA with the classical, direct democracy of Athens and the European tradition. De Tocqueville expressed concerns that American republican democracy was open to two potential dangers. On the one hand, the potential for autocratic control or excessive influence of particular groups was present because of the lack of traditions and constraints in the new country. In contrast, there was the possibility of reduced power of elites in favour of a form of popular democracy in which public opinion would play a major influence. The question was whether the USA could steer a course between these two potential dangers and develop a form of liberal democracy that would grant personal freedoms and political engagement while retaining the capability to govern a vast territory, a diverse population and a dynamic economy. These questions took on a renewed importance in the 1940s and 1950s partly in response to post-war reconstruction and partly because of America's new place in the world.

Milgram was interested in the theoretical question of the relationship between the capacity of individuals to assert their rights and bring authority to account and the politics of democratic society. However, Milgram became convinced that empirical social science had a lot to say about the nature of political participation and engagement. In contrast, he was disconcerted by the way, that political theory appeared to rehearse intractable oppositions between conservative and liberal theory. This concern with the way that individuals coped with the responsibilities of being citizens as an empirical question was one of the main reasons why Milgram shifted from political science to social psychology. Blass (2004) argues that this decision was a radical turning point in Milgram's life as he moved away from the abstractions of political theory and embraced empirical social science. However, Milgram never lost his interest in social and political theory and so was particularly attracted to the interdisciplinary research context of the institute for social relations at Harvard in which sociologists, social anthropologists, psychologists and political scientists worked together, across disciplinary lines to address the main issues of contemporary American society.

In addition to these personal commitments, which drove Milgram towards an empirical social psychology with political engagement, he grew up at a time when questions of power, authority and political participation had great importance. The period following the Second World War at the time that Milgram was a student of political science and developing his ideas on social psychology was an interesting time in American politics reflecting the broader social changes discussed in the last chapter. Blass (2004) documents that Milgram felt increasingly out of sympathy with political radicalism in the late 1960s, an era when political struggle found expression through direct action and university campuses were often the front line of protest and confrontation. While Milgram was opposed to the Vietnam War and nuclear armament, he was not in sympathy with violent protest and direct action; he was a liberal and wanted to change the political system through argument and discussion rather than through violent confrontation. However, perhaps there was also an intellectual issue for Milgram here, for the actions of student radicals and proponents of the protest movement flew in the face of his theories of obedience to authority. What was emerging was a form of collective action against authority and a general scepticism and distrust of political authority culminating in the impeachment of President Nixon in 1974. The actions of protesters and the general collapse of deference and trust in authority discomforted and perturbed Milgram because he viewed obedience as necessary for the good society.

In the early 1970s, when Milgram was writing *Obedience to Authority* the cold war had erupted into the real war in Vietnam. Milgram documents some of the atrocities committed by American soldiers such as the My Lai massacre in which US troops killed villagers including children and non-combatant adults. He makes the parallel between the trial of the soldiers for this massacre and the trial of Eichmann in order to emphasise his central point that the psychology of individuals does not fit them well to stand against power. He argues that the actions of individuals in the extreme circumstances of war and totalitarian political regimes are part of the same psychology of the obedience to authority exhibited by political conformity and by the participants in his experiments. The early 1960s, when Milgram was conducting his obedience experiments, was the height of the cold war between the West and the regimes of Russia and China. I will outline some of the key issues and themes of the cold war and domestic politics in the US to flesh out the context in which Milgram conducted his experiments before discussing the links between his studies and questions of political theory.

Debates in political theory about what was the best model of democratic government for the USA reflected these real world issues. Some advocated a restricted conception of the political sphere in which citizens consent to grant power to elected representative and administrative elites. In contrast, others advocated a pluralist democratic culture in which a variety of sources of power compete and balance each other so that no single power or authority could dominate. For the advocates of elite democracy, political engagement was mainly restricted to voting while pluralist theories argued that political participation was much broader, encompassing membership of social movements, groups and institutions. Milgram hoped that his experiments into obedience to authority would address these themes of political psychology and participation by demonstrating how citizens respond to authority.

I will explore three themes in this chapter, which reflect on the political dimensions of Milgram's research. First, I have argued that the context of post-war American political culture influenced Milgram's social psychology so I will flesh out that context and show how it influenced Milgram's concerns and his studies. Second, Milgram's research reflects on a longstanding debate in democratic theory about freedom. Is democratic freedom attained by reducing constraints on personal freedom or by developing the context for individuals to realise their potential as citizens. Finally, I will link Milgram's work to the key debate of his day between advocates of elite democracy and of pluralist participatory democracy.

## Post-war US political culture

### The Cold War

In the period that Milgram was a student and conducting his research on obedience to authority, the USA was involved in a conflict with the USSR referred to as the 'Cold War'. At the time of the Second World War and in the post-war period, Russia was the largest of a number of nation-states that together constituted the Union of Soviet Socialist Republics (USSR or the Soviet Union). This was a vast 'empire' of socialist states including Russia, the Baltic States and the southern states such as the Ukraine and Georgia. During the Second World War, the USA and the USSR were allies fighting against and ultimately defeating Nazi German and its allies. However, although they joined forces against Fascism, the USA and the USSR were very different states. The USA was a liberal democracy with a dynamic capitalist economy and the USSR was a federation of socialist states with a command (state run) economy. The two allies were ideologically, politically, socially and economically opposites and after the war they were the two remaining world superpowers. Tensions emerged between the two even before the end of the Second World War and as both were ambitious imperialist states, the post-war world was characterised by conflict as each tried to assert world domination through military, economic and political means. This conflict was the Cold War, which had important effects on American political culture.

In his excellent book *The Cold War*, Gaddis (2005) draws out the differences in political culture in the USA and the Soviet Union in 1945, the immediate aftermath of the Second World War. Although both superpowers were powerful countries that had their origins in revolution, the political systems that emerged from those revolutions were radically different:

> The American Revolution, which had happened over a century and a half earlier, reflected deep distrust of concentrated authority. Liberty and justice, the Founding Fathers had insisted, could come only through constraining power ... The Bolshevik Revolution, which had happened only a quarter century earlier, had in contrast involved the embrace of concentrated authority as a means of overthrowing class enemies and consolidating a base from which a proletarian revolution would spread throughout the world (Gaddis, 2005, p. 7).

The USA had emerged from the Second World War as a great world superpower; militarily successful, economically dominant and with a political system that claimed to deliver unprecedented personal freedom. However, as Gaddis points out, the end of World War II did not create a stable global political environment but instead a sense of competition, insecurity and threat. Hitler's Germany was defeated but new threats emerged in the shape of the Soviet Union and Communist China. America's problems were not restricted to foreign affairs. There were many problems in the USA arising from the lack of financial and life prospects, political representation and influence of many individuals due to '...the legacy of slavery, the near extermination of native Americans, and persistent racial, sexual and social discrimination' (Gaddis, 2005, p. 7). Many citizens felt politically free but unequal in rights and access to the fruits of victory.

Abroad, the USA embarked on a global conflict with socialist regimes that would lead to war in Korea and Vietnam accompanied by the massive development of its nuclear armoury and the threat of 'mutually assured destruction'. Simultaneously, at home there was growing protest and social conflict over the rights of individuals in the human rights movements of the 1950s and 1960s. The state responded vigorously to the internal troubles just as it had to the external threats from state socialism. An important part of this response was the rapid development of the Central

Intelligence Agency (CIA) in the post-war years. The CIA had only 302 employees in 1949, but grew to 2,812 by 1952 with an additional 3,142 overseas agents (Gaddis, 2005, p. 163). A key issue surrounding the increasing covert operations of the CIA abroad was that their actions, including subversion, assassination and propaganda, contradicted the principles of American democracy in which the powers of governments should be limited, visible and accountable; here was an agency that acted under conditions of secrecy and deniability outside the control of elected representatives. An argument in favour of covert operations was that the Soviets were able, because of their autocratic political regime, to deploy spies, assassins, subversives and propaganda to undermine regimes favourable to the USA and that a response in kind was required.

One response to the perceived external threat to the USA from socialist regimes was an enhanced role for the CIA operating outside the principles of public accountability. However, since the threat was partly perceived as internal, resulting from the actions of spies and radical political activists, and the agency worked against internal enemies in secret, how could the rights of US citizens be guaranteed? The possibility that covert operations would take place in the USA itself aimed at its citizens created a new threat to their freedom. The clandestine operations of intelligence agencies combined with a series of public events, highlighted the supposed 'internal threat' from those with radical political sympathies. For example, a little known Senator Joseph McCarthy began to make a series of public denouncements of widespread communist sympathisers in the government, administration and public life.

McCarthy's accusations tapped into and amplified the sense of vulnerability and insecurity engendered by the Cold War. In 1952, McCarthy became chair of the Permanent Investigations Subcommittee and launched a series of inquiries into government officials and public figures. Films were made of the hearings of the committee and broadcast on Television. The representations of the committee were highly salient at the time and helped to establish a climate of fear and suspicion, the sense that individuals in the USA were under surveillance and that anyone with subversive or left wing views was vulnerable to public accusation, loss of their job and even imprisonment. Although McCarthy was soon discredited, he had fed the mood of fear and accusation and reinforced the impression that the state had taken new powers of authority in which it released agencies to work on its behalf without supervision beyond the reach of public scrutiny to protect the democracy whose principles it violated. McCarthy brought home to people the idea that these powers might be used against them, that in the apparently benign conditions of post-war liberal democracy they might be subject to powers that one could expect to operate only in a totalitarian regime. Big Brother was supposed to be a parody of the Soviet Union but appeared to be happening at home.

Other cases reinforced the idea that spies and communist sympathisers had infiltrated the USA and that liberal democracy was vulnerable because of its openness and tolerance. The conviction for espionage and consequent execution by electric chair in 1953 of a couple called the Rosenbergs was another iconic event which appeared to demonstrate that some US citizens had been recruited by the soviets and justified covert actions against Americans. Zinn (1980) argues that the evidence against them was highly suspect, that the witnesses were mainly spies and criminals and that the judge in the case did a deal with the prosecution against the interests of justice. Whether the Rosenbergs were guilty or innocent victims of covert action, they were a highly salient example that both strengthened the idea that the USA was under threat from communist infiltrators whilst reinforcing the idea of the vulnerability of the public to accusation. Further:

> In that same period of the early fifties, the House Un-American Activities Committee was at its heyday, interrogating Americans about their Communist connections, holding them in contempt if they refused to answer, distributing millions of pamphlets to the American public: 'One Hundred Things You Should Know About Communism' ('Where can Communists be found? Everywhere'). Liberals often criticized the Committee, but in Congress, liberals and conservatives alike voted to fund it year after year... Although Truman criticized the Committee, his own Attorney General had expressed, in 1950, the same idea that motivated its investigations: 'There are today many Communists in America. They are everywhere – in factories, offices, butcher shops, on street comers, in private business – and each carries in himself the germs of death for society' (Zinn, 1980).

Arthur Miller expressed these concerns through his play *The Crucible,* which told the story of a group of hysterical teenagers in 1692/3 New England accusing citizens of witchcraft and sorcery, which in the hands of enthusiastic ministers of the church led to the hanging of innocents who would not admit their guilt or fault. Miller's play is a brilliant allegory that uses a cultural form to interrogate the McCarthy hearings, exposing the vulnerability of individuals to the combination of the authority of the state and the cruelty of one person against another. We can interpret Milgram's experiment in the same way as an expression of the lack of constraint on state power and the consequences for vulnerable individuals enrolled as agents of the state against their fellow citizens. The experiment works as a political allegory as much as a forensic, scientific analysis of behaviour.

On top of all this, the atomic bomb changed warfare irrevocably and brought with it the potential threat of war to destroy cities, nations, populations and even the planet. The Bomb was a new source of anxiety for citizens of the USA. US forces had suffered casualties in Europe during the Second World War but America had avoided the massive civilian loss of life and extermination experienced by Europe and Japan. The destructive power of atomic weapons and their capacity to reach and destroy cities in the USA potentially eclipsed the horrors of the Second World War. The atomic bomb was a key component of the USA's military domination at the end of the Second World War, ending the war with Japan. The Bomb also expressed the dominance of American science, technology, economic power and political will to defend the nation. As the USSR developed equal destructive capacity, what had once been America's triumph now became its biggest threat. A deadly arms race to develop weapons of mass destruction between the US and its new enemies ensued.

In addition, as Gaddis notes, the political regime of the Soviet Union under Stalin, although presiding over a devastated empire, was full of purpose and menace. The Soviet Union was reproducing the Nazi's mixture of state control, terror and propaganda allied to military and political strength. In contrast, democratic regimes appeared weak, lacking in direction and full of contradictions (Gaddis, 2005). Britain and the USA lost their wartime leaders shortly after the war whereas Stalin consolidated and developed his power base. The idea developed that America might be drawn into a nuclear war that had the potential to reach mainland USA and that the hearts and minds of the American people might be open to influence from insidious propaganda and the infiltration of open society by agents of socialist regimes. The ironic and dangerous point was the belief that these dangers were partly the result of the freedoms granted by the American political system.

Gaddis suggests that these uncertainties went to the heart of US foreign policy creating the tension between the idea that republican democracy would provide a model for the rest of the world to follow and the idea that America was bound to become the policeman of the world in order to make it 'safe for democracy'. This oscillation between isolationism and imperialism was unresolved in the development of nuclear military policy; was it to protect the homeland or to stop the spread of alternative (socialist) ideologies across the world?

These factors lead to the contestation of fundamental rights enshrined in the Constitution and a renewal of the debate over the power of the state. Should America go forward in pursuit of equality and the rights of citizens or did the state need to take powers to produce political agreement and conformity in order to counter the potential threat from the Soviet Union and China? This was the period when the young Stanley Milgram was being educated at university, taking his degree in political science and then his doctorate in social psychology and ultimately designing and conducting his studies of obedience to authority.

## The CIA and human experimentation

Milgram's experiment was an expression of concern at the state of post-war political culture in the USA. However, it also reflects some of the actions of the CIA during this period on the home front. In addition to seeking out spies, insurgents and fifth columnists and publicly humiliating individuals who were alleged supporters of communism, the CIA sponsored a good deal of psychological and medical research into the suggestibility of individuals and the limits of individual self-determination. In these studies, experiments explored the potential for brainwashing and mind control using psychological techniques and hallucinogenic drugs. On one level, this was an attempt to develop new, sophisticated techniques of interrogation and torture. On another level, it was part of the response to the use of such techniques on captured US servicemen by communist regimes and the suspicion that propaganda had successfully influenced susceptible individuals in the Western World. In response to moral panics about the infiltration of American society by subversive agents and messages, a range of experiments were conducted to examine the ways in which individuals could be manipulated and controlled. The CIA introduced this programme partly in response to the use of brainwashing techniques on US prisoners of war in Korea as a result of which prisoners appeared on film making extraordinary confessions and denouncing their government for its involvement in the war. This climate of fear was dramatised in the (1959) film *The Manchurian Candidate* in which a group of American prisoners of war were brainwashed so that they would return to the States as assassins targeting political leaders.

In her 2007 book *The Shock Doctrine* Naomi Klein provides a dramatic account of one of the victims of a programme sponsored by the CIA and the Canadian government in the 1950s which:

> ... funded a Montreal doctor to perform bizarre experiments on his psychiatric patients, keeping them asleep and in isolation for weeks, then administering huge doses of electroshock as well as experimental drug cocktails including the psychedelic LSD and the hallucinogen PCP (Klein, 2007, p. 28).

Klein links this kind of experimentation to two themes: the destruction of an individual's personality, motivation and self-control by psychological techniques of torture rendering them open to suggestion and the implementation of neoliberal economic policies in response to crises in America and abroad. Klein describes the covert operations of the CIA as 'the CIA's thirst for information about the control of the human mind' (Klein, 2007, p. 28). The doctor in charge of the Montreal experiments, Ewen Cameron, used multiple electric shocks combined with mind-altering drugs to disorient, disrupt the memory and to regress his patients to a childlike state. This made them receptive to a series of taped suggestions, which told the disoriented patients such things as 'You are a good mother and wife and people enjoy your company' (Klein, 2007, p. 32).

Klein documents that the CIA invested $25 million in research projects to explore different methods of disorienting and then 'refocusing' participants. She describes the distribution of funds to a variety of research institutions, universities and hospitals between 1953 and 1963. The CIA programme enrolled eminent psychologists and medical researchers to conduct research into the conditions under which individual self-control could be weakened or broken and therefore open to suggestions. A well-known example is Hebb's research into sensory deprivation in which individuals were isolated and their senses masked by goggles and white noise. This disoriented the participants and made them open to influence from ideas that they had previously objected to, demonstrating the potential for social influence on vulnerable subjects (Klein, 2007).

Milgram's obedience research shares many of the features of the experiments conducted and funded by the CIA as it explores the limits of self-determination, uses an emotionally charged method to disorient participants and the commands of the experimenter to control and influence their actions. In a recent book, *A Question of Torture*, Alfred McCoy (2006) suggests that the CIA covertly funded Milgram's experiments into obedience to authority. Milgram's biographer Alan Blass and Milgram's collaborator Alan Elms strongly deny these claims (See Blass's website: www.stanleymilgram.com). However, whether or not the CIA funded Milgram, it is clear that his experiments resonated with the CIA's interests in the psychological limits of autonomy and the conditions under which individuals would follow suggestions or instructions. In addition, the use of deception, disorientation and electric shock were all common in CIA sponsored research. It is at least the case that Milgram's experiments caught the spirit of the time and articulated the threat to the autonomy and identity of US citizens in the late 1950s and early 1960s.

## Post-war political culture

These events and conditions were clearly in Milgram's thoughts as he decided to specialise in the psychology of social influence. His political sympathies were liberal (Blass, 2004) and his concerns were with the potential excesses of authority and the potential of the public to resist the political excesses of the state. Milgram's personal reflections on the Holocaust heightened his concerns about the developments of techniques of social control, the increasing power of the state and the conformity of the public. I will give a sense of Milgram's experience by drawing on Todd Gitlin's book *The Sixties: Years of hope, days of rage*, which does an excellent job of setting the scene in the late 1950s and early 1960s in the USA from the perspective of someone with a Jewish background growing up in New York before going to university. Gitlin argues that one feature of the political culture of the USA in the 1950s was that the conservative political settlement was constantly being questioned by counterculture movements that often found expression in culture, art, movies, and literature. His analysis suggests a paradox in American culture: that it combined unprecedented affluence with deep insecurity.

Once the war was over, consumer demand was a dynamo. Industry and government as never before channelled capital mobilised Science.

> The boom was on, and the cornucopia seemed all the more
> impressive because the miseries of Depression and war were
> enough to suffuse the present with a sense of relief (Gitlin, 1987,
> p. 13).

The American dream of opportunity in a land of plenty appeared to be on the threshold of being realised. The demography of America was changing because of the baby boom, the population moved from rural to urban centres and from urban centres to the new suburbs (Gitlin, 1987). The suburb became the symbol of the new prosperity and the site for the development of consumer culture with the family as the primary social institution: the nuclear family with father working and mother at home became the ideal and the reality for this affluent generation. The suburbs needed the car and the supermarket transformed shopping. The car became the vehicle of choice 'the incarnation of personal power, freedom, leisure, sex, access, efficiency, ease, comfort, and convenience all wrapped up in a single machine' (Gitlin, 1987, p. 16).

> For the multitudes who could afford the ticket, then, the payoff for
> hard work and a willingness to accept authority promised to be a
> generous share in the national plenitude (Gitlin, 1987, p. 16).

The new medium of television carried images of mind control and torture, the Bomb and the McCarthy hearings into the homes of American families. These were very powerful symbols that shaped people's sense of isolation persuading them that the dangers they faced that were out of their control and that powerful forces might have devastating consequences on their lives. Gitlin tries to express the power of the feeling of nuclear Holocaust in the lives of ordinary Americans during this period:

> Children who grew up in the Fifties often dreamed, vividly,
> terrifyingly, about nuclear war...To some extent it must have been the
> stress of amply reported East-West confrontations. As the air raid drills
> confirmed, the Bomb was not just a shadow falling on some distant
> horizon. Bombs were actually going off. H-bomb tests obliterated
> atolls in the South Pacific; A-bombs regularly scorched the Nevada
> desert (Gitlin, 1987, pp. 23–24).

During this time, there was an explosion in popular culture genres such as sci-fi and horror that depicting isolated American communities succumbing to external or internal physical threats and psychological terrors. Against this background of fear and uncertainty, Gitlin suggests that the public reflection on the Nazi Holocaust took a particular form in the 1950s, which fed into the sense of threat and fragility of the post-war settlement:

> For Jewish adolescents in particular, the Nazis were not long defeated, and Hitler the most compelling of bogeymen. 'Camp' did not mean a place to go for the summer. Protective parents were reluctant to remind us, but rumors and images and random facts did seep into our consciousness. Photos of camp survivors, not yet stereotyped, floated through popular culture like stray bones, and lodged, once in a while, in our collective throat…The Holocaust had not yet acquired that name, at least in my hearing; the catastrophe was simply a mangled piece of history, incomprehensibly real, unique to the twentieth century; our century (Gitlin, 1987, pp. 24–25).

Milgram was one of those adolescents and his ideas and reflections combined in the way described by Gitlin as a set of concerns about the Nazi Holocaust and the threat to the republican ideals of US democracy. The participants in Milgram's experiments were living through times which both granted unprecedented opportunities and freedoms in the context of a social formation that dispersed and isolated them as individuals in an affluent society under the threat of extinction from abroad and surveillance at home.

These features of the political culture of his time bring into question one of Milgram's favourite claims about his experiments: that the people who turned up to do his experiments were ordinary people not disposed to obedience except through their biological nature and not prone to mental health problems that might cause them to bring harm to others. If the features of the political culture of the late 1950s and early 1960s had any influence, then the people who walked through Milgram's door were citizens of a political culture that had offered them a social contract that traded affluence for social isolation, anxiety and conformity. The individuals who completed Milgram's experiments reflected this culture. They were looking for experience but deferential, self-confident but aiming to fit in and sensitive to threats, conscious of their rights but fearful of authority. They represented the new individuals of the modern world whose moral obligations to others were in flux as were many things in their society.

## Political freedom

Milgram's obedience experiments reflect a discussion in political theory during the 1950s concerning the nature of liberty or freedom. In 1958, Isaiah Berlin wrote an essay in which he identified two approaches to freedom in political theory: negative and positive freedom (or liberty) (Berlin, 1969). Negative freedom refers to the constraints or coercion that might form obstacles to the actions of free individuals (Carter, 2007). On this view, people are free to the extent that there is an absence of such obstacles or constraints. In contrast, accounts of positive freedom focus on the capacity and opportunities for individuals to develop qualities such as autonomy, self-control or self-realisation. Milgram's obedience experiment contains features that demonstrate the operation of both negative freedom (the constraints of the experimental context and the influence of the experimenter, which led to obedience) and positive freedom (his account of the possibility of individuals exercising autonomy, following their consciences and disobeying authority). The choice that Milgram created for his participants operationalises the distinction between negative and positive freedom. The experiment asked whether individuals would express positive freedom by disobeying the experimenter or demonstrate the way negative freedom constrained their conduct through obedience.

At first sight, therefore, Milgram's experiment appears to be a straightforward test of these rival theories of politic freedom. The high levels of obedience in the experiment demonstrated that there was a problem of negative freedom because people were susceptible to social influence, which constrained their freedom to act. However, the freedom that they were unable to express was the positive freedom of realising their autonomy and resisting authority and the reason that Milgram claims that they were unable to do this is because they were in a suggestible psychological state. Remember that the experiment demonstrates social influence rather than coercion. Milgram's experiment celebrates positive freedom, reflecting Fromm's influence.

However, in political theory negative freedom usually refers to external factors bearing down on the individual and positive freedom to internal, psychological factors. While most would agree that negative freedom is a political question since the degree to which individuals are constrained, influenced or coerced by external powers is critical to their freedom, the situation is not so clear for positive freedom (Carter, 2007). Positive freedom seems more a question of political psychology than political theory. The argument is further complicated because usually when political philosophers advocate positive freedom they are thinking about the individual joining in collective action. However Milgram's experiment removed the potential for collective action by isolating individuals. Milgram adopted an individualist conception of positive freedom and consequently, the solution that he advocates is a combination of removing social pressure on individuals thereby enhancing negative freedom and encouraging their capacity for self-determination and self-realisation through raising awareness thereby enhancing positive freedom. Milgram appeals to authority to constrain itself and thereby to create the conditions under which individuals can develop autonomy.

However, Berlin (1969) advocating that liberal democracies focus on negative freedom by granting freedoms of movement, religion and so on, warning of the dangers of institutional involvement in positive freedoms. The legacy of the Holocaust and the claims of state socialism influenced Berlin just as it had Milgram. As Carter suggests:

> Berlin, himself a liberal and writing during the cold war, was clearly moved by the way in which the apparently noble ideal of freedom as self-mastery or self-realisation had been twisted and distorted by the totalitarian dictators of the twentieth century (Carter, 2007).

Berlin argued, based on events in Nazi Germany and the Soviet Union, that when states get involved in questions of positive freedom they take a position on what counts as both rational and free. The consequence is to divide the political subject into the acceptable and the unacceptable so that certain ways of thinking, feeling and behaving are valued over others and in the name of positive freedom. Milgram, even though he restricts himself to an individualistic conception of positive freedom nevertheless also divides the political subject in two, represented by those who obey in the agentic state and those who disobey because they act with autonomy and conscience. Milgram values one of these states (autonomy) over the other (the agentic state), thereby privileging a particular way of acting. However, we must be careful because he used these arguments not to press the claims of a particular ideology or collective but to offer a warning of what he thought was happening in liberal democratic society. In addition, his proposed solution, linked to pluralism, is that political institutions should make sure that they create the conditions under which individuals can grow and take responsibility for them. Milgram takes the view that the conditions in which individuals can develop positive freedom in their choices depended on a variety of sources of advice and guidance so that no single source of authority can dominate. Elites can legitimately guide and influence people's lives in the context of pluralism because they can never gain sufficient power to dominate.

## US political theory in the 1950s

What were the implications of Milgram's sensational findings for American democracy? At the time when he was a student, the debate about what form political institutions should take in order to manage the complexity of liberal democratic rule and enable personal freedom was being discussed. Two theories contested these questions by advocating an elite democracy and a plural, participatory democracy. I will discuss these two theories of liberal democracy and relate them to Milgram's obedience experiments in this section.

### Competitive elitism

Weber's ideas had a strong influence on one of the main theorists of competitive elitism, Joseph Schumpeter (1976). Schumpeter argued that in modern industrial societies the complexity of social and economic processes means that it is not feasible to grant political control to citizens. It was appropriate that citizens had specific and restricted political role, best exemplified by voting, in which they express their opinion as a public and based on which they give over the right to govern to a political elite. Schumpeter argued that the impracticality of direct democracy in large-scale, complex modern societies and the empirical realities of public disengagement, fragmentation and irrationality in liberal democracy also supported the idea of elite democracy. Assumptions that citizens are active political agents are central to liberal democratic ideals:

> Central to the whole liberal tradition has been the notion of human beings as 'individuals' who can be active citizens of their political order and not merely subjects of another's power (Held, 2007, p. 153).

Schumpeter allowed that individuals in post-war USA were active participants in the sphere of their private lives where they exercised choice as members of local communities, families and as consumers, but he did not think of them as active participants in the political sphere beyond expressing their preferences through the vote. Milgram's experiments, on the face of it, give support to Schumpeter's ideas by illustrating individuals' deference to authority and trust in social institutions. However, Milgram's participants were deferential to a university professor conducting an experiment, suggesting that deference and conformity had spread well beyond the political sphere. Either the acceptance of political power was widely generalised to cover dispersed forms of authority or acceptance of political authority reflected a broader culture of conformity. Milgram's results do not support Schumpeter's view that trust and consent in the political sphere complement freedom and autonomy in the private sphere.

Schumpeter argued that minimal participation in politics through voting would be sufficient to make citizens of modern complex societies accept political rule. He argued that if people voted then they were expressing their agreement to the political order and were happy to cede political power to the party or person that won the election. On this view, a general lack of political participation is not a sign of apathy and lack of political agency but of trust in and contentment with their rulers. Held (2007) suggests that Schumpeter underestimated the different meanings behind the apparently general consent given by people who voted in elections. People can interpret voting in a variety of ways. They may believe that they had no real choice, were following tradition or apathetic. They may have preferred an alternative but pragmatically go along with the choice in front of them or that although they were dissatisfied they vote in order to improve things. They might agree with the politics and actions of those they are voting for, or that the people they were voting for genuinely represented their values and interests (Held, 2007).

Applying these distinctions to the Milgram experiment we can see that some of these descriptions do apply to the participants but others do not. For example, it is conceivable that the obedient subjects in Milgram's experiment felt that they had no choice, that they were supporting the traditions of the university and science. Some may have been apathetic. Others might have liked an alternative but decide to go along with the arrangements. Other obedient participants may have gone along with things even though they were dissatisfied (and some of them expressed this through their complaints and expressions of concern). However, it is difficult to find evidence in Milgram's writings that his participants agreed with the actions of the experimenter and felt that they represented their own vales and interests. Some of Milgram's participants were obedient but they did not legitimate the actions of the experimenter. Indeed, they found a variety of tactics to signal their lack of agreement and their concern. These were not the contented consenting citizens of Schumpeter's account of political subjects in liberal democracy.

The participants in Milgram's experiments represent the state of political engagement in the USA in the early 1960s; they combine deference and passivity in the face of authority with political discontent. Milgram was a liberal not a radical and he conducted his experiments as a warning, that mainstream political culture had become a culture of conformity. However, in this interpretation Milgram followed Schumpeter in overstating the degree of consent, not recognising the way that his participants signalled their concern and tried to bring authority to account and giving insufficient attention to the many who disobeyed in the experiments. Milgram's participants did reflect a time of deference and conformity but they also anticipated the more radical politics that emerged in the late 1950s and early 1960s that was about to erupt in the protest and life political movements of the mid to late 1960s but which were below the surface during the time that Milgram was conducting his experiments.

## Pluralism

The rival political theory in the USA in the 1950s to Schumpeter's competitive elitism was pluralism. According to pluralists, elite theorists had underestimated the ways in which private individuals were connected to the political process through membership of civil society bodies such as trades associations, trades unions, religious bodies, community associations and interest groups (Held, 2007, p. 158). Held explains that theorists in the pluralist tradition such as Dahl (1956) argue that the purpose of government in modern society is to create conditions in which a diversity of groups can pursue their political interests and to make sure that no particular group dominates. A plurality of groups competing for power and influence is seen as the basis for stability in complex societies as groups adopt a variety of different resources to push their case; some have access to money, some to education, while others have the power of social connections. The ideal of a pluralist society is to establish conditions in which all of these interests have a voice so that particular interests do not dominate.

This characterisation of the 'realities' of political influence in the post-war USA suggests that power is non-hierarchical and dispersed across different social groups and formations. Individuals are not isolated in the face of power as suggested by Schumpeter, but members of diverse groups with different resources and access to power. It is through their membership of plural collectives that individuals influence the political sphere, not as isolated individuals. Milgram's experiment isolated individuals from their social context: the workplace associations, clubs, societies and community groups through which they might meet their political objectives. This suggests a further layer to the deception in the Milgram experiment. Participants might have reasonably assumed that the university and the practices of social scientific research were institutions that would serve and protect the public. Participants volunteered their time on the assumption that they were contributing to a public knowledge project. They were aligning themselves, temporarily, to a public institution but when they arrived and as the experiment proceeded, they found themselves subject to isolation and pressure.

Milgram's experiment demonstrates what happens when individuals are cut off from their communities, friends, associates and affiliations and subjected to illegitimate authority. This supports the idea that resistance to authority depends upon social connection and a plural political culture. The capacity of individuals to resist power is radically diminished when social connection and capital is diminished. Milgram's work also supports pluralism because it represents an academic intervention in social and political debate. A healthy democracy, according to pluralism, consists of the influence of institutions and bodies in civil society able to represent the interests of different, often minority, viewpoints to political leaders and foster engagement and compromise. This view informed Milgram's conception of his role as a public intellectual who could contribute to public discussion of the dangers of political culture and thereby serve the interests of the public. The demonstration of the vulnerability of the political subject was an intervention by an expert and academic in social psychology in public debate. Milgram claims his role and the context of the university as an active institution of civil society from which he can legitimately challenge and influence public debate by conducting and publicising research that addresses social, political and moral concerns.

## Conclusions

As a work of political psychology, Milgram's experiments on obedience to authority raise a number of fundamental questions about the political agency of citizens of liberal democracy. The actions of free citizens in the experiments reflect the political culture of their day, they were deferential but concerned, express distress and dissatisfaction but are intimidated by authority. As a performative demonstration, Milgram's experiments are rich and open up a range of interesting questions about the social contract of modern democratic society. However, Milgram's hopes of resolving long-standing disputes about political subjectivity through empirical testing fail. As with the social questions that his experiments raise, the design of his experiment is not neutral but structured by his assumptions about political psychology, which were derived from his reading of political theory and his social concerns rather than providing an adequate test (even if such a thing were possible) of the psychological assumptions of political theories. The value of Milgram's experiments is in the way they provoke and remind us of the complexities of questions of political subjectivity, power and engagement.

Milgram's experiments also afford reflection on the nature of freedom in liberal democracy since those who were obedient demonstrated the power of social influence to limit freedom and those who disobeyed were heroic representatives of positive freedom in the exercise of their autonomy and self-determination. Milgram demonstrated through his experiment the relevance of social influence to questions of freedom supporting a broad conception of politics and the constraints on freedom. Furthermore, his work demonstrates the centrality of social relations and people's beliefs, desires and values to an understanding of their capability to act freely and protect themselves from social control.

# 6 The Individual in a Social World

Milgram is perhaps the best-known social psychologist outside the discipline and he and his experiments are a fantastic ambassador, bringing the issues and concerns of the relation between the individual and the social world to a wide audience. Many praise Milgram for his creative use of the scientific method, his engagement with both sociological and psychological theories, and his courage in tackling issues of real social, political and moral concern. Milgram offers us an image of social psychology as a unique area of study between sociology and psychology. On this view, social psychology is different from individual psychology in that it seeks to understand the relationship between social conditions and feelings, thoughts and behaviour. It is also distinct from sociology in that although it addresses social conditions, the focus is on the experience of individuals.

Milgram's work also demonstrates that social psychology is an insecure territory, sitting between two academic disciplines and borrowing theories and methods from both. At the extremes, the gap between sociology and psychology is large; the neurological end of psychology and the study of the state in sociology are not easy to integrate. However, the psychology of beliefs or values and sociology focused on social interaction in institutions and everyday life offers a more plausible connection. Doing social psychology is not a simple matter of combining elements of sociology and psychology because social psychologists have to make assumptions about which aspects of the social are relevant, which psychological phenomena they are concerned with and how to manage the relationship between potentially incompatible ways of thinking about human beings: the social and the individual. To put the problem at its bluntest, do we accept an image of human beings as pre-social, as defined by their biology, their character and the individual circumstances of their lives and then subject to a variety of social influences? Alternatively, do we think of human beings as inherently social; brought up in families and other social groups, subject to social influence from a young age and that this interacts with and influences their psychology over time?

In this chapter, I will discuss Milgram as a social psychologist by exploring the empirical work that he conducted on other topics after the obedience to authority studies. Milgram collected these together in his book *The Individual in a Social World*.

## The Individual in a Social World

In 1977, Milgram published his book *The Individual in a Social World* in which he gathered together reports of the different areas of social psychological research that he had conducted over his career including a chapter summarising the obedience to authority research. The titles of the book's chapters represent the other areas of research that Milgram had engaged in: the individual in the city; the individual and the group and the individual in a communicative web. These areas of study, along with the individual and authority indicate that the key theme of Milgram's social psychology was the orientation of the individual to a variety of social groups and institutions.

As we have seen, Milgram believed in the importance of the individual as the focus of social psychology and was concerned about the exposure of the individual to the powerful social influences in the modern world. He believed that individuals were comprised of character and various behaviours that reflected their biological heritage. In his empirical work, he aimed to gather moments of social action, snapshots that revealed the balance of power between the individual and society. His basic approach was to ask how individuals adapted and oriented to their social world, drawing on the resources of their character and taking into account their biological make up. He took these ideas, worked out as he designed his obedience experiments, into his other empirical studies in social psychology. Milgram was a social scientist, but in addition, he was a filmmaker and social observer with political and social concerns and he brought this sensibility to his research.

Milgram starts *The Individual in a Social World* with the following statement:

As a social psychologist, I look at the world not to master it in any practical sense, but to understand it and communicate that understanding to others (Milgram, 1977, p. 1).

Milgram believed that good social psychology emerges from the experience and reflections of the investigator on their own experience as social actors. What makes social psychology a social science is the application of systematic ways of studying the social world guided by personal experience and reflection in order to gain understanding that might be of use to others. This is a humanist and pragmatic notion of the value of scientific knowledge; that it is a refinement of ordinary experience, grounded in the personal experience of the investigator, appreciative of the spontaneity and pleasure as well as the challenges of being a human being living in a social world. Milgram sets himself the task of conducting systematic, scientific studies focused on the practical problems of modern living in order that he might find out about the social world in a way that will generate understanding that will make it possible for people to live better lives.

Milgram aims in his empirical studies to capture both the subjective experience of living in a social world and an objective analysis of social conditions that provide the context for social action. The appreciation of human experience requires empathy, interpretation and theory, and the understanding of the objective social world requires observation and experimentation guided by insights from social and political theory. Social life, then, for Milgram is composed of two interpolated orders: subjective experience and objective social order. For Milgram these two orders are integral aspects of the human condition. Of particular interest to the social psychologist, according to Milgram, are the discrepancies between our subjective experience and the objective facts of our social environment: the gaps between the subjective and the objective, between people's experience and the facts of their social environment. For Milgram this is what social psychology is about: exploring and coming to understand subjective experience and then understanding the way that our beliefs, attitudes and values, our view of our place in the social environment falls short of or differs from the way that the social environment is organised in ways that can cause problems for people. Milgram argues for the need for social psychology to play a role in providing knowledge and expertise arises from the discrepancy between people's self-understanding and the facts of their social environment.

## The individual in the city

Milgram begins his account of his various studies of living in cities by lamenting the lack of social psychological work on this topic. Social psychologists prefer to explore the experience of being in small groups and he challenges us to explore the relationship between the individual and broader social formations. As he points out, the city is a key social formation that provides the context within which many people live out their lives and he raises a challenge: can social psychology include an analysis of social institutions and structures whilst retaining its focus on the experience and actions of individuals? Milgram presents an agenda for potential social psychological work in studying the individual in the city. Using New York City as his example, he observes that people often comment on the frenetic, high-speed life of the city and wonders if social psychologists can find a way of measuring the meaning of the experience of the pace of life. Milgram discusses the cities he has lived in: Boston, New York and Paris. Intuitively he feels that the experience of living in these cities is different and he sets himself the task of capturing the subjective experience of the city by using social psychological methods.

Milgram undertook two kinds of empirical work on the experience of living in the city. He got students to conduct a range of experiments on the streets to discover inhabitants' reactions and he examined the cognitive maps that people had of the cities they lived in. Starting with the idea of measuring the experience of living in a city, Milgram got his students to conduct a variety of experiments comparing the behaviour of individuals in urban and small town settings in the USA. For example, he sent students into the street and asked them to greet strangers by offering to shake their hands, in urban settings 38.5% of people shook hands compared with 66.7% in small towns (Milgram, 1977). He explained this difference by suggesting that population density overloads the individual making them less open and friendly to others. However, he suggested to some degree the positive excitement of living in very large cities such as New York compensates for these negative effects. Milgram's students also conducted a study of 'the familiar stranger' in which they photographed individuals in the morning who were commuting on the train into the city of New York. The students subsequently showed these photos to other commuters and were able to demonstrate that although people describe themselves as strangers in the city, they could recognise the commuters who regularly shared their journey.

This research is characteristic of Milgram's later research. The papers mainly report data gathered as part of his teaching and comprises fascinating glimpses of the social psychology of the city rather than constituting a systematic programme of research. The appeal of these small pieces is the way in which Milgram identified original and intuitively appealing topics of research and the creative approach to research methods adopted by his students. Milgram sent his students out into the streets to participate in and observe moments of interaction in the city that were often surprising or against the grain of normal social behaviour. Milgram and his students were like a street theatre troupe engaged in public participation and they would then return to the university to interpret their results. In this work, Milgram demonstrates the sensibility of an ethnographic filmmaker and, as with his obedience research, his explanations come in the form of diverse, intuitive reflections informed by theory rather then systematic theory development.

Milgram performed two studies of the psychological representations of the city: one in New York and one in Paris. In New York, he showed 150 photographs of views from across the city and asked people to say which of the scenes in the photographs they recognised. He then built up a 'recognition map' of New York City showing, for example, that Manhattan was the most recognisable borough and reinforcing his idea that there are two orders (the objective and the subjective) that together form the experience of living in the city. For Milgram the difference between the maps normally produced by cartographers and his psychological maps of recognition was the starting point for a psychology of the meaning of the city for its inhabitants.

However, his maps of recognition disappointed Milgram; it was interesting to see the areas that people recognised but the maps did not capture the meaning of the city for its inhabitants. In response, Milgram designed a study of psychological maps of Paris, carried out in collaboration with Serge Moscovici and Denise Jodelet. In these studies, Milgram got 218 residents from different areas of Paris to draw maps of their city. What emerges is that people are familiar with the idea of representing their own psychological perspective on the city and that their maps were both realistic and unrealistic. They were realistic in that the general shape of the city and location of key landmarks was often recognisable, although some people drew schematic diagrams. However, what is clear is that people drew the maps to represent their ideas about the city. Some referenced the complex mix of the old and the new architecture that characterises Paris, others drew detail on parts of the map, for example of their own neighbourhood. The maps linked detailed sections to the well-known landmarks of the city, mixing the private and the public just as living in the city mixes private and public aspects of social life. Other maps were topographically inaccurate but represented plausible sequences of landmarks drafted to represent the narrative of walking through the city. Others were idealised maps of what people would like the city to be such as the city of the future.

Serge Moscovici and Denise Jodelet's work on social representations influenced Milgram's interpretation of the common elements across the maps drawn by individuals. He observed that although the maps often had idiosyncratic elements, together they constituted a shared social representation of the city. This social representation included the general shape of the city, the construction of the boundaries of the city, the location of key historical monuments such as Notre Dame and the river Seine represented as a gentle arc through the city rather than the more meandering course it actually takes. The gentle arc of the river was so common across quite different maps that it appears to have the character of shared public knowledge, derived from cultural representations of the city and shared amongst the inhabitants. Allied to the centrality of the Seine to the social representation of Paris is the importance of the key, central monumental architecture of the city, with Notre Dame to the fore. In contrast to New York, which has more dispersed landmarks, the maps represent Paris as grounded in its ancient architectural monuments; the social representation refers to tradition and religion as at the core of the meaning of Paris to its inhabitants. Milgram summarises his interpretation:

> Such maps are multidimensional. They contain cognitive and also emotional and intuitive components ... the maps are not individual products; they are shaped by social factors, and therefore acquire the status of collective representations – that is, symbolic configurations

of belief and knowledge promoted and disseminated by the culture (Milgram, 1977, p. 89).

In Paris in 1972 to 1973, Milgram was falling under the influence of the city and the ideas of Moscovici, derived from Durkheim's arguments that what appear to be psychological phenomena, such as beliefs, attitudes and feelings, are often expressions of a shared culture. Milgram was writing his book *Obedience to Authority* at this time, yet he did not bring the ideas he was engaging with about collective dimensions of social experience to bear on his deliberations on obedience. Consequently, Milgram presents us with two very different accounts of relations between individuals and society in his obedience work and in his work on the social representation of the city. In the obedience experiments, the individual is alone in the face of extreme and immediate social pressure. In contrast, in his studies of the meaning of the city, he suggests that psychological experience is often part of a representation of a shared culture, powerful representations that nevertheless are adaptable to individual experience.

What are the themes of Milgram's diverse studies of living in the city? Milgram demonstrates that the cities that people live in are psychologically real for them, an important part of their experience. People see themselves as individuals who are a small part of a much larger social entity. His studies demonstrate that subtle rules of conformity establish the level of communication and engagement that we have with our neighbours and fellow urban inhabitants. Objectively the city establishes a range of conditions that alienates and separates individuals, leading to a picture of the individual lost in the crowd. But, Milgram identified a range of ways in which people cope with the overwhelming complexity with which a large city confronts them: they 'make sense' of the urban environment by developing their own psychological maps of the city, reducing complexity and making the city have personal meaning for them. A culture of shared representations and experiences links individuals to their fellow citizens. Individuals also develop a range of tactics, such as being familiar with strangers, so that they are moving through the city with people like themselves, creating a sense of belonging to a group even though they might never talk to their fellow travellers.

In all this, Milgram is suggesting that our social environment shapes our psychology in two distinct ways. First, the social environment is a real force that directly impinges upon us in a variety of ways: forcing us into close contact with others, to follow routines and paths through the complexity of the city, sweeping us up in the energy and flow of city life. Second, in response to these ways that social forces in the city impinge upon the individual, people have developed a range of psychological tactics to ameliorate the potentially negative effects of urban life. They live within a psychologically manageable part of the city, adopting routines to handle the exposure to the potentially alienating presence of strangers and making the city psychologically meaningful as a representation.

## Crowds

Milgram's studies of the city developed new techniques to capture experience, but his approach to social psychology also required him to develop methods of mapping the social environment to contrast with subjective representations. Milgram developed this as part of an essay on the crowd in *The Individual in a Social World*. He aimed to develop an external, objective view of the crowd by examining aerial photographs of crowds forming in a Moroccan marketplace. An advantage of photographs taken from the air is that they are an unobtrusive measure; individuals are not aware of the observer and so one of the biggest criticisms of the obedience studies, that the experimenter influenced the outcome does not apply. In his analysis of the photographs, Milgram notices that the movement of people through the marketplace forms into a pattern of circles around traders. The circles are relatively stable structures but have permeable boundaries as people move through the marketplace stopping to gather round one trader, then another. Milgram contrasts these emergent structural characteristics of crowds to the idea of a chaotic mob that comes out of Le Bon's work on the crowd. In contrast to the mob, the crowd in the marketplace formed a fluid but relatively stable and ordered system. Milgram observes that people play out different roles. Some individuals are at home in the crowd, in tune with its energies and flows. Others are prepared to go along with the suggestions that emerge from the crowd and take on the anonymity that the crowd offers. There are passive individuals energised into action by the crowd and others who support the crowd but remain relatively passive on the edges of the action. Finally, there are individuals who are present but resist the persuasive influence of the crowd adopting the attitude of observers or witnesses.

Milgram outlines and criticises Le Bon's (1999) analysis of the crowd and in particular draws out Le Bon's argument that the crowd could sway the rational individual toward irrationality. Milgram is ambivalent on this point, for as we have seen he believes that gatherings of people have a number of 'rational' or at least organised features. He does not see social gatherings as necessarily a rabble. However, Le Bon influenced Milgram's analysis of the obedience experiments, in that he saw rational behaviour as individual (the conscience and self-control of the individual who would not want to harm others). Also, obedience resulted from the individual disengaging their self-restraint and rationality in the face of social pressure and acting in a less thoughtful, more intuitive and responsive fashion. As in much of Milgram's work, he opened up rather than resolved these questions and contradictions.

Milgram had other reasons for thinking through the sociology of the crowd beyond these questions of social psychological theory. The actions of crowds were significant for Milgram writing in the mid-1970s because by then the student protest and life political movements of the 1960s and 1970s appeared to contradict many of the implications of his work on obedience to authority. All over the world, there had been protests against the conformist and conservative regimes of the 1950s and against the growth of corporate capitalism. Furthermore, apparently contradicting the results of the obedience experiments, the protests took the form of direct political action more reminiscent of the participants in Gamson's research on group disobedience than Milgram's obedient subjects. How would Milgram respond to this apparent shift in the public appetite for disobedience?

Milgram reflects on these issues not by engaging directly with these social changes but through a discussion of the academic work of Lipset and Wolin (1965), which analysed the Berkeley student protests of 1964. They describe how tensions arose between students and the university administration over the authorities' decision to deny the right to hold public political meetings on campus. The students responded by holding sit-ins (occupying university buildings) and protests involving hundreds of students which hundreds of the police dispersed through violent confrontation. Milgram draws on Smelser's (1963) theory of collective behaviour, in turn influenced by Parsons' social theory of action, to explain the student protests. Milgram applies Smelser's idea that collective action results from shared beliefs and coordinated action aimed at changing the social environment.

Milgram adopts Smelser's argument that six factors determine what form collective action will take. Smelser regards these factors as interdependent, but not necessarily realised as a sequence. First, 'structural conduciveness', which in the case of the student protest is the transparent difference between students and the university authorities, the formation of shared views amongst the student group about the need for change, the commitment to freedom of speech, the gathering together and communication within the student group and the lack of alternative means to express grievance. Second, 'structural strain', refers to the growing tensions between different collectives, in this case the students and the university authorities. Third, 'growth and spread of belief', refers to the development of shared beliefs amongst a collective about the causes of the strain they were experiencing and the agreement on a plan of action. In this case, the student body recognised that the authorities had denied their rights and that they could demand them back through protest. Fourth, 'mobilisation for action' occurs as the result of the actions of student protest leaders actively encouraging dissent and protest. Fifth, 'precipitating factors' or the spark needed to provoke action, in this case the announcement of the removal of the right to assembly on university property. Sixth, 'social control' refers to the way in which various social agents encourage or discourage collective action. In the case of the Berkeley protests, the authorities and police discouraged student protest but the faculty and student organisations advocated collective action (Milgram, 1977).

Milgram points out that Smelser's analysis derives from Talcott Parsons' analysis of social systems as combining the levels of social systems, culture and personality. The social system is a system of social roles prescribed by shared social norms and underpinned by shared values. Parson believed that shared values reflected in common beliefs and shared meanings that were found in any culture were the basis of social order. Personality refers to the systematic internalisation of motives, emotions and beliefs in individuals. The students' actions arose from an alignment of threats to a social group from another part of the social system, the formation of shared values within the student body and personal commitments to action. In this interpretation of protest in a student movement Milgram attempts, as he did throughout his career, to explain social behaviour as only explicable by combining sociological theory with social psychological analyses of social events and behaviour.

Surprisingly, Milgram explains the student protests as conformity and obedience to authority rather than as disobedience. This demonstrates how far Milgram was prepared to go to support his functionalist view of society and his conception of individuals as mainly obedient and passive. He argues that the academics and the student leaders established themselves as the authority to which the students deferred. Milgram's discussion of sociological explanations of student protest misses an important aspect of his work on social influence because the protest movement provides graphic evidence that runs counter to his theory of obedience to authority: here was social disobedience in the form of collective action.

In all this, we can see the clash between the liberal progressive humanist views that had motivated Milgram's approach to social psychology and the emerging radical social movements of the 1960s and 1970s. Milgram's vision of a protective liberal democracy in which the vulnerability as well as the freedoms of individuals was recognised and his preference for elite, benevolent leadership was potentially undermined by the rise of social conflict and more radical politics. Instead of the difference between liberals and conservatives within which Milgram had framed his political and social project, new terms of debate over liberal governance were emerging in which neoliberals and social democrats were rethinking the issues and formulating new conceptions of governance and political subjectivity. I will return to these issues in the next chapter when I examine the contemporary reflections and resonances of Milgram's work.

## The individual in a communicative web

A theme of my analysis of Milgram's social psychology is the influence of Parson's structural functionalism on his thinking about the relationship between people and societies. Part of the Parsonian analysis of social systems was the importance given to culture interpreted as a system of shared values, beliefs and symbols. As a social psychologist, Milgram adopted this interpretation of culture but focused on how the individual experiences culture. He was also aware, with great prescience, of the changing nature of culture in the USA. The mediation of culture shifts the orientation of the person to society. In his obedience experiments, Milgram argued that authority in contemporary society was symbolic. The authority of the experimenter arises from the way that he symbolised various aspects of modernity: science, technology, education, and modernisation. In modern societies culture is increasingly mediated through the culture industries rather than emerging from the actions and shared understandings of individuals.

Milgram was amongst the first social psychologists to understand the growing importance of communication for social and individual life. This was at a time when much psychological work on communication adopted metaphors from engineering and was concerned about signal and noise and communication as the flow of information. On this, as in so many things, Milgram was idiosyncratic and had his finger on the pulse of important developments in society and the broader social sciences. If the natural environment of human beings is living in small groups and communicating face-to-face, then for Milgram there were major difficulties for individuals orienting to society with a dispersed, large scale population that get a sense of their shared beliefs and values from the media. Milgram saw these issues as the problem of being an individual in a communicative web needing to contact individuals through the network of social relations in contemporary society and to connect to systems of mass communication.

## The small world problem

In indigenous societies, social interaction connects individuals to everyone else in their community through face-to-face communication. Milgram's work on living in cities demonstrates that for much of their time in public, individuals in the modern world are in the company of strangers. People live at a distance from their friends and families, their homes separated from their work rather than part of the same social space. Modern societies are complex, multilayered networks of interconnection between large numbers of people. However, Milgram assumed that the need for association with other people was basic to the human condition, raising the question of how people can maintain their social relationships (with family, friends or colleagues) given that modern life separates people. It would be easy to be pessimistic about the potential for connection between people enmeshed in a network society. However, as we have seen in many of his studies, perhaps with the exception of the obedience experiment, Milgram believed that people have adapted to the gap between their psychological needs and the circumstances in which they live in the modern world. Milgram's social psychology first identifies these gaps and then examines the strategies and tactics that people develop to overcome the problems of modernity. Therefore, he looks to see if there are strategies of connection that people have developed to overcome the social distance that potentially results from the complex communication networks and social differentiation that characterise the modern world.

Milgram outlines the possible positions on this problem as an opposition between pessimists and optimists. Pessimists think that the complexities that arise from the loose interconnection between millions of people mean that the individual is doomed to a life of isolation. In contrast, optimists think that human beings can find their way through the complex networks that constitute modern culture. Milgram, as is his way of approaching such questions, is a realist about the complexities and difficulties presented by the modern social world but an optimist about the capacity of people to overcome these problems. Milgram reviews some of the work done on social network analysis applying the mathematics of graph theory to a variety of applied social science problems.

Graph theory was applied to the analysis of logistics to work out the best path through a network. For example, a haulage firm providing goods to supermarkets in a city has to traverse a complex network of streets to visit a sequence of stores. The mathematics of graph theory enables the calculation of the shortest pathway that connects all the supermarkets to minimise the amount of driving needed to complete the deliveries. The social psychological question is whether the same rules that govern spatial dispersal of objects in physical space apply to the psychological space of connections between individuals. Michael Gurevitch (1961) in his doctoral dissertation had applied these methods to the analysis of sociometric data in which people kept a record of everyone that they met over a period of 100 days. Gurevitch's analysis showed that people were in contact with about 500 other people and that the chances that any two people have a mutual contact is as high as 50% whereas the pure probability of any two people in the US being connected is 200,000:1. In other words, the practical ways in which we live our lives, in family and friendship groups, our neighbourhoods and workplaces creates a radical simplification of social networks. In addition, individuals' networks are partially overlapping so that it is best to understand the country as a whole not as on huge network of millions of individuals but as a network of networks, each of about 500 people.

Milgram suggested that because it is both possible to find efficient pathways through social networks via mutual contacts and that social connection is a network of networks, that there should in fact be quite short links between any two people in a society. In contrast, if a society were a vast network of individuals, the links between people through acquaintance chains would be very long indeed. Milgram, the creative empirical researcher, designed a procedure to test the theory of efficient social networks. He gave the name and address of a target person to participants and asked them to get a message to the target person using only direct connections through networks of friends or acquaintances who were asked in turn to contact their networks of friends and acquaintances until the person is reached. Milgram conducted two studies, in which participants in the Midwest of the USA (Wichita, Kansas and Omaha, Nebraska) were sent the name of a target on the East coast (Boston) and asked to contact the person through their friends and acquaintances using a chain letter technique.

The first letter arrived at the target person's address in Boston from Kansas in days, illustrating how the small world problem is resolved in practice. Milgram gave participants in Kansas the name of one of the two target individuals, the wife of a divinity school student in Cambridge, Massachusetts. The first letter to reach the target was from a farmer in Kansas who had passed it on to his local Episcopal minister who in turn passed it on to a minister he knew who taught in Cambridge and who in turn knew the target and was able to pass on the letter. This path through the social network used only two intervening links! This is a particularly impressive example, however, on average people only needed 5.5 links to reach the target person. Therefore, although people were geographically and socially remote from the target person they were able to use their network of acquaintances to pass on the letter to relevant contacts in their own networks to find a person who was a direct acquaintance of the target person (Milgram, 1977).

Milgram collected and analysed the chains of connection and showed that there were more same sex than cross sex contacts and that people sent more letters to friends and other social contacts than to relatives. The findings as a whole show that individuals are not embedded in society as a whole but in the small world of their network of friends and acquaintances. Closer inspection of the last link in the chain showed that three people were key bridging points between the target person and networks outside his small world. These key links were also from different domains of life: work, neighbourhood and a shopkeeper in the target's town. This demonstrates that not all links are equal but that certain key individuals in our small world connect us to the small worlds of others. Each of the average of six links represents their own 'small world' or social network demonstrating that it is not simply a link between five people but the overlap between six social networks that connects individuals together through social relationships. Individuals appear to have a rich source of social contacts that link them to the broader society; this resource of social contacts is social capital (Putnam, 2000). Milgram's study demonstrated neatly that the connections between networks of individuals were an important dimension of communication in a complex modern society and that the social capital of individuals varies in that some are more central to networks of communication than others.

Milgram's work on the small world problem demonstrates many of his strengths as a social psychologist. He took an established issue in social psychology, the study of interaction in small groups and local communities and had the creativity to adapt it to the larger scale issues of communication in a modern society. It also demonstrates his commitment to the idea that human beings have the capacity to find practical solutions to the problems of living in modernity. In addition, Milgram had again put his finger on the pulse of what was to become a major area of study in the sociology of communication: the study of social capital (Putnam, 2000).

## The lost letter technique

The discrepancy between attitudes and behaviour is an acknowledged problem in social psychology. The classic study of LaPiere (1934) demonstrates that even racially prejudiced individuals who worked in restaurants and hotels do not refuse service to people from ethnic minority groups, illustrating that there is a gap between attitudes and behaviour. Social psychologists often conduct research using survey and interview techniques in which they depend upon people being prepared to say publicly what their attitudes are. This is a problem if the topic they are trying to find out about is personally or politically sensitive or offensive because there is likely to be a gap between the attitudes that people express and their behaviour. Milgram developed the lost letter technique as an unobtrusive method of getting a sense of public attitudes without having to ask people to state their views publicly. He developed the technique as part of one of his graduate research seminars in which he and his students dropped stamped letters on the streets of New Haven. Each letter had similar, innocuous content, but the addresses were significantly different: one version was addressed to the *Friends of the Nazi Party*, one to the *Friends of the Communist Party*, one to *Medical Research Associates* and one to a fictitious individual *Mr. Walter Carnap*. All of the addresses used the same post office box and address in New Haven, Connecticut. The letters were distributed in different areas of the town and sealed so that on return the researchers would know which letters had been opened and read. The post box belonged to the researchers and they waited for the return of the letters. Seventy percent of the letters to both the research institute and the private individual were returned but only a quarter of the letters to the friends of the Nazis and Communists. The point is that on a topic on which it would be difficult to get people to express their opinions openly and publicly, the lost letter technique allows people to express their views through their actions in an unobtrusive, unobserved fashion.

Having established that the technique worked, Milgram and his colleagues applied it in different contexts. They demonstrated the strength of feelings over race relations by finding that different letters were returned from communities with different ethnic mixes. In political psychology, Milgram used the method to study the 1964 presidential election and the returns accurately reflected local patterns of voting. The lost letter technique has often been used as an unobtrusive measure in political communication and reveals Milgram's creativity and optimism that key issues in social psychology (in this case the gap between attitudes and behaviour) can be overcome through innovative design in empirical studies. The substantive point that Milgram's studies demonstrate is that it is not always possible for participants to express opinions in public, a topic subsequently developed in the study of the spiral of silence in political communication (Noelle-Neumann, 1993).

## Television and antisocial behaviour

In *The Individual in a Social World*, Milgram has a chapter reporting an empirical study on the effects of television. The exploration of the effects of television has a long history in social psychology and is an area of considerable controversy and debate. However, in the early 1970s, when Milgram conducted his research, there was optimism that social psychology could make a considerable contribution to answering important social questions about the potentially positive and negative effects of television.

Milgram presents a review of some important studies of the effects of television. He describes Gerbner's (1972) cultivation analysis that used content analysis to measure the level of violent content on TV, which showed that there was far more violence in the world of TV than in the 'real' social world. Gerbner and his colleagues correlated levels of TV viewing with subjective estimates of levels of violence and negative social attitudes such as fear of crime. The key finding is that those who watch more TV tend to endorse the 'mean world syndrome' represented in the content of TV rather than public statistics on the levels of crime. Watching TV appears to acculturate individuals to the world as represented on TV rather than the real world that they inhabit. However, Milgram is not impressed with Gerbner's findings because they only tell us which viewing habits are associated with certain beliefs and so do not tell us whether the media causes people to be fearful or whether fearful people tend to watch more TV.

Milgram also gives a negative review of Bandura's famous 'Bobo Doll' experiments demonstrating that children will imitate aggressive behaviour towards a toy doll that they had previously observed in a film. Children who had seen the film were more likely to attack the doll themselves in a play session than those in control groups and they imitated the behaviour of the adult in the film. Milgram is critical of the lack of direct relevance to everyday life (eco-validity) of Bandura's experiments, which did not use recognisable media content, nor a realistic context of viewing. Milgram is also critical of the Himmelweit et al. (1958) surveys of families and children in the UK because surveys can only provide correlations and not identify causes. However, Himmelweit et al.'s (1958) study did include a natural experiment, as they were able to study homes before and after the introduction of TV coverage.

Milgram was impressed, however, by a naturalistic study conducted by Feshback and Singer (1971), a summer camp study in which one group of boys was exposed to a violence-rich media environment (they were shown films with many violent episodes) and another group was exposed to media with less violent content. The results suggested a cathartic effect, as the boys exposed to the greater violent media content were less aggressive when observed during their time at the camp than the boys who had viewed less violent media content. The argument is that viewing violent content does not lead to imitation but to a release of violent tensions and frustrations, contrary to Bandura's thesis that exposure to violent media content leads to imitation. Milgram's review of previous studies of media effects reflects his views about the importance of the experiment as a method in social psychology. Although he is committed to conducting research that addresses social issues and takes into account social theory, his preference is for experimental methods. His criticisms of previous research in media effects focus on methodology and ignore the care and theoretical sophistication of the work of Gerbner, Bandura and Himmelweit. His review also ignores the debates in the sociology and psychology of media on the complexities of the relationship between media, culture and society.

In his own research on media effects, Milgram designed an elaborate study, which in one phase used a cinema in New York to display different versions of a hospital soap opera professionally produced by a media company. One version of the programme presents an individual aggressively robbing charity collection boxes using a baseball bat. After viewing the programme, participants entered a holding area, which contained such boxes. Researchers observed them using closed circuit TV to see if they would be aggressive and rob the charity boxes. The study was a complete flop, none of the manipulations worked; the design was poor, suffering from similar issues of eco-validity that Milgram had used to criticise Bandura. The manipulation of violent media content was simplistic and crude and the context of viewing was unrealistic; who watches a soap opera in a cinema? Milgram seems to have not taken onboard some of the main difficulties of researching the effects of television, which mean that an experimental approach is limited in value; that TV effects are diffuse, take place over a long period, mediated by viewers' beliefs and practices. The crude manipulation of violent media content also fails to recognise the acknowledged difficulties in defining media violence. Not surprisingly, given all these issues of theory, design and interpretation, Milgram's experiment was a complete failure. The principles that had served him so well in his obedience experiments of drawing on his sensibility to a social problem and designing an experiment to capture the key issues failed to provide him with a successful strategy in his media effects research.

## Conclusions

Milgram made significant contributions to the study of social influence, social capital and research methodology in social psychology. Throughout his research career, he maintained his commitment to develop a socio-logical social psychology focused on the problems faced by individuals living in modern society. His approach was grounded in his personal experience, reflected the breadth of his reading in the social sciences, and placed a high value on the capacity of empirical research to test the psychological assumptions of social and political theory and to provide insights and information that were of public value as well as academic interest. Milgram achieved all this with a great deal of intelligence, style and humanity. He was a performer, inspiring his collaborators and students to conduct creative empirical studies that raised important questions and provoked debate. However, Milgram was rooted in the problems of the liberal democracy of the USA in the late 1950s and in both his theoretical and political commitments he was increasingly out of touch with social and political developments and intellectual trends. Despite this, paradoxically, his intelligence and creativity as a researcher generated highly influential research that still resonates today, as we will see in the next chapter.

Contemporary Resonances of Milgram's Research

## Introduction

Why does Milgram's research, particularly *Obedience to Authority*, still fascinate us today? The value of the research as science is only a small part of the reason for its continuing relevance. It must be that Milgram expressed in his experiments a number of themes, dramatically evoked by the setting and the behaviour of the participants that captured important social, moral and political questions. In previous chapters, I suggested that one reason why the experiments are so full of meaning is that Milgram was open to the influence of a range of theories and ideas from sociology and political theory. These theories addressed important issues of the nature of individuality, power and political engagement in modern society while simultaneously reflecting on the evocative and important concerns surrounding the Holocaust and the conditions of life in liberal democracy.

Certain questions still resonate on hearing about the findings of the obedience experiments: would I have done the same thing as the participants? Does obedience to authority challenge our views about the nature of moral agency? Could individuals in contemporary society resist a malevolent authority? Are individuals in modern liberal societies as vulnerable as the behaviour of Milgram's participants suggests? What implications does this have for our understanding of the Holocaust and the operation of power? Milgram's research does not answer these questions in a forensic, scientific sense but opens them up for reflection, discussion and debate in the same way that a good play, film or novel does.

The way that his ideas have been taken up in a variety of academic disciplines such as social psychology, political science, sociology and Holocaust studies illustrates the diversity and range of questions raised by Milgram's work (see Blass, 2004, for a review). However, the experiments have captured the public imagination beyond the boundaries of academia. Blass

(2004) documents how Milgram's obedience experiments have become part of popular culture reflected in songs such as Peter Gabriel's 'We do what we're told (Milgram's 37)' on his album *So*. Conceptual artist Rod Dickinson presented a detailed stage re-enactment of the Milgram experiments at the Centre for Contemporary Art in Glasgow in 2002. A number of plays have been written inspired by the obedience experiments including Dannie Abse's play 'The Dogs of Pavlov' (Blass, 2004). Like a film or a book, Milgram's experiment offers a setting and a cast of characters and allows the action to unfold as a narrative offering us the chance to think through general questions of human nature and society.

In this chapter I will explore the discussion of Milgram's findings in writings in the history of psychology, moral theory, sociology and media studies which creates an impression of the manifold interpretations afforded by his research. The intellectual range of these questions also reflects Milgram's eclecticism. We read Milgram today through the lens of the way that subsequent writers take up, rework, contest and elaborate the underlying questions and concerns in his work. This sharpens the analysis of the assumptions made by Milgram in framing and writing about his research. Conceptions of what counts as critical social science, of individuality and individualism, of the morality of virtue and of the operations of power have all changed significantly since Milgram's day. What is remarkable is that the experiment still challenges and discomforts us.

## Individuality and individualism

One of the features of Milgram's work that gives it continuing relevance was that he insisted on treating the individual as an important social entity and believed that the best way to comment on the state of American society and democracy was to ask what experiences and issues individuals faced in the contemporary world. This was a controversial position in his day and it remains controversial today. In the 1930s, the idea of putting the experience of the individual at the centre of social enquiry was challenged by the increasingly scientific approach of psychology, which either delved into universal psychological processes without recourse to experience and individuality or studied aggregated data from surveys, thereby also dispensing with the need to understand personal experience. Milgram stood against these trends. Today the idea of the individual as the basic unit of explanation in the social sciences is questioned both by scientific psychology that examines intra-individual psychological processes, by radical social psychology that criticises the humanist assumptions of traditional social psychology and by sociology where methodological individualism has been widely criticised.

An important feature of Milgram's experiment was that he isolated individuals and cut them off from the outside world. In contrast to theories of social influence that emphasise the individual as part of a crowd or group, Milgram saw social influence as the impact of social forces acting on the individual and obedience as dependent on whether the individual had the resources to resist social pressure. Milgram expresses this in the preface to his book *The Individual in a Social World*:

> The late Gordon W. Allport taught that social psychology examined how the thought, action and feelings of the individual were affected by the implied, actual, or imagined presence of others. At the centre of his definition was the individual: the individual remains at the center of my own conception of the field (Milgram, 1977, p. vii).

What were the origins of Milgram's commitment to the individual as a social entity and the basic unit of social psychological analysis and research? We can trace some of these ideas back to two important influences on Milgram's work. One derives from Weber's analysis of the emergence of the modern individual in the reformation and Fromm's reworking of these ideas in *Escape from Freedom*. The second derives from the commitment of Gordon Allport, Milgram's supervisor, to an approach to social psychology that had emerged in the USA in the 1930s as part of the attempt to reconstruct American society in the wake of the Great Depression. In her book *Rebels within the Ranks*, Katherine Pandora (1997) presents a detailed analysis of the work of Milgram's supervisor and mentor Gordon Allport along with his colleagues Lois and Gardner Murphy. The debates and ideas of Allport and the Murphys provided an influential context for Milgram's work. Pandora explains how Allport and the Murphys developed radical commitments during the 1930s in which they came to the view that social psychology should play a twin role in challenging the status quo of both science and society:

> That historical, economic, and political questions played themselves out within personal and social worlds suggested to Allport and the

Murphys that psychological research could be used to critique American culture and thus to help create a more democratic polity (Pandora, 1997, p. 3).

The critique of the application of natural science to social science went hand in hand with the critique of the state of US democracy and was influenced by the pragmatist philosophy of John Dewey who had asserted that '*social* cannot be opposed in fact or idea to *individual*. Society is individuals-in-their-relations. An individual apart from social relations is a myth – or a monstrosity' (Dewey and Childs, 1935, cited in Pandora, 1997, p. 5). Allport adopted the idea of studying 'the-individual-in-social-context' (Pandora, 1997, p. 5) as a way of opposing the focus on psychological generalities at the expense of the study of individual psychological experience. The emphasis on social context was also a critique of the move towards scientific psychology, which regarded human beings as objects of study rather than reflective social agents. This pragmatist orientation was also critical of the positivist separation of different academic disciplines because understanding the human subject as an individual needed the combined efforts of anthropologists, psychologists, sociologists and the arts. In all this, Allport and the Murphys were placing themselves in direct opposition to the dominant development of behaviourism, which applied natural science principles to the study of behaviour. Milgram was the direct inheritor of this tradition. As is clear from the title of his book *The Individual in a Social World*, Milgram adopted a range of observational techniques and natural experiments that come close to the prescriptions of Allport and the Murphys for a return to a naturalist orientation to research as opposed to experimental manipulation. When he did conduct experiments, in the obedience studies, Milgram left open the outcome and collected evidence about participants' experiences to complement the measures taken.

Pandora traces the intellectual legacy of Allport and the Murphys to William James's radical empiricism and his contribution to the development of pragmatism as a philosophical position. The contestation of the idea of truth as an inherent property of ideas and the adoption of the idea that truth resides in events or process is an important part of pragmatism. The argument is that it is better to judge the character of individuals through their actions just as the motions of objects reveal the operation of physical forces. The influence of this idea on Milgram is clear in the way that he set up his experiment not as a forensic examination of the qualities of character but as a context in which events would unfold and be open to interpretation to discover the truths about obedience.

Another important reason for the focus on the individual and experience was to counter the tendency in scientific psychology to break the social and the psychological into its constituent parts. In contrast, Milgram placed the experiencing subject at the centre of his experiment. He manipulated the social context but allowed the individual subject to follow their own path through the experiment and recorded their experience. Allied to this, Pandora argues, 'that James, as a *public* philosopher, believed that intellectuals bore a fundamental responsibility for bringing their academic work to bear on public problems', (Pandora, 1997, p. 24). There could be no better commentary on Milgram's commitments to an empirical psychology that puts human experience at its centre, regards truth as revealed through events and is oriented to social issues.

Another way in which Allport's and the Murphys' adoption of radical empiricism influenced Milgram was in their commitment to treating individuality as both a political and a scientific problem (Pandora, 1997, p. 63). These writers linked philosophical and methodological commitment to individuality to a radical democratic political perspective. Scientific psychology seemed complicit with the eradication of the individual from the social and political environment; a movement that radical democrats of the 1930s resisted by asserting the centrality of the individual to democracy. However, it is important to recognise that Allport and the Murphys were advocating individuality in a social world, not individualism. Milgram's normative project in conducting his empirical social psychology is to preserve, protect and support the individual in the modern world.

Milgram was also influenced by Allport's and the Murphys' ideas of how to articulate the embedding of individuals in social context. Their first point was that it is not possible to apply a pure scientific orientation to understanding the social context within which individuals lived and instead they advocated 'impure science'. That is they 'assumed that their endeavour was indeed a social exercise, and that science was, as a result, shot through with moral and political values' (Pandora, 1997, p. 90). Milgram was an advocate of 'impure science' embedded in the broader intellectual climate of his day and focused on real world issues. The generation of radical social psychologists that preceded and taught Milgram anticipated many of the key issues in Milgram's research. The focus on the individual, the attempt to understand individuality in social context, the vulnerability of the individual as a key problem of modern democracy, the importance of immanent social and political purpose in social scientific research, the need to connect social psychological questions to those of sociology, anthropology and other social sciences.

## The Third Reich in power

One of the motivations of radical liberals in the USA in the 1930s to pre-serve the political status of individuals came from their reflections on emerging totalitarian regimes in Germany and Russia. The threat in these countries to the individual through a combination of terror and persua-sion was an important motivation for the focus on the individual in social psychology that Milgram inherited from critical theory and social psy-chology. Evans (2006) analyses the link between the self-proclaimed national socialist revolution and individualism as expressed in a quote from Goebbels in 1933: '[in] ... the transformation of the German nation into one people ... the era of individualism finally died ... The individual will be replaced by the community of people' (Evans, 2006, p. 120). Linked to this was the way that the revolutionary interests of the state would extend far beyond the '... political sphere. From there they reach out to cover all areas of human existence. The economy and culture, science and scholarship, and art are not protected from their impact' (Goebbels, 1933, cited in Evans, 2006, p. 120). To carry out this revolutionary purpose, Hitler established the Ministry of Popular Enlightenment and Propaganda under Goebbels aimed at the 'spiritual mobilisation of the German people' (Evans, 2006, p. 121). As Evans explains:

> Of all the things that made the Third Reich a modern dictatorship, its incessant demand for popular legitimation was one of the most striking. The regime put itself almost from the very start in a state of permanent plebiscitary consultation with the masses (Evans, 2006, p. 121).

Evans (2006) is in no doubt about the cynical nature of this mass pro-paganda that constructed a compliant and adoring public and thereby created the conditions under which individuals would feel constrained about expressing their private concerns about the Nazi regime and in which other potential political parties and leaders would feel intimidated. Evans documents the techniques of social influence that aimed to enrol the individual to the purposes of the state. Ritual events such as the annual Nuremburg rally were part of a construction of tradition that supported the cult of personality built up round Hitler. Evans details the fantastic logistical effort in staging the 1934 Nuremberg rally in which five hundred trains transported a cast of thousands to a specially built railway station. A city of tents housed thousands who participated in an orchestrated series of events over a week, culminating in an affective effervescence of quasi-religious ritual and ceremony at Hitler's address. Evans (2006) describes how the grand ritual ceremonies, filmed and shown across the country were supported by the practical efforts of Goebbels's ministry. In these practical, mundane, but no less important ways, Hitler was praised in speeches and articles, supported by a variety of decrees that spread the ritual deference to Hitler as father and leader in the Hitler salute which inserted commitment to the regime in the practices of everyday life in a display of deference.

Milgram encoded elements of this familiar story of the way that the Nazi regime came to hold the German nation in thrall before leading them to disaster into the design of his experiments. The idea of a hierarchical and conformist social order with an implied consensus of obedience played out in the interaction between authority figures and members of the public inducing an emotional dependency in participants that reduces their ability to act as autonomous individuals. Milgram's response is to work as a public intellectual, promoting public awareness and the reinvigoration of autonomous, committed individuals.

We can question whether Milgram's idea that obedience to authority reflects the early signs of totalitarianism was justified and whether his proposed solutions of the bolstering of the individual and the commitment to pluralist forms of knowledge and expertise as a way of reinvigorating public engagement in politics and guarding against threats to liberal democracy. Evans's (2006) analysis of the role of propaganda in the early days of the Nazi regime demonstrates that the popular plebiscite of the early Nazi regime replaced both the individual as an autonomous political entity and public opinion in the form of a naturally occurring consensus both of which were central features of 1950s liberal democracy. This was not a value consensus but the internalisation of a set of norms and practices organised around a vocabulary of spirit, nation and the articulation of those who were part of and excluded from the nation. Arendt's call for vigilance of extensions of power in liberal democracies accompanied by scepticism towards popular democracy and media-managed public opinion influenced Milgram's work.

Milgram, influenced by critical theory, took the concerns that arose from the comparison between liberal democracy and totalitarian regimes and focused it on the disenchantment that accompanied the new social and political landscape of post-war America. If what distinguished liberal democracy from tyranny was the freedom and ability of citizens to make independent political judgements and to make civil commitments through engagement with social and political issues, then isolation and fragmentation, apathy and alienation would allow elite power to operate without appropriate checks and balances. However, as Evans's (2006) analysis demonstrates, the Nazis linked a totalitarian regime to the manipulation of popular legitimation. Public opinion, instead of being the expression of the will of the people became a means of bending individuals to the political will of a fascist regime. The same concerns were circulating in postwar America that consensus was a reflection of conformity and apathy rather than the expression of agreement among free individuals. Milgram as a liberal humanist placed great importance on the individual as opposed to the mass of public opinion as the appropriate locus of consensus and legitimacy. However, one reading of Milgram's experiments is that under conditions of pressure from authority it is extremely difficult for people to assert their autonomy and call authority to account. Milgram's political commitment was to pluralism; to offer the public an alternative understanding of their role as political subjects so as to disrupt the normative pressures of authority and to encourage and support the autonomous critical subject to assert their individuality and bring authority to account.

## Power and subjectivity

Milgram's experiment represents the power of authority and the deference of the subject as the two sides of the coin of domination. In addition, influenced by Weber and critical theory, Milgram defined power as the interaction between social institutions and individuals, hegemony results from the domination of subjects by institutional power and freedom equates with the autonomous expression of individuality in the face of authority. Consequently, the health of a democracy resides in the capacity of free thinking, autonomous subjects to give their consent in the political sphere, thereby forming consensus on political issues legitimating the institutions of the state and acting freely in the private sphere. Milgram is committed to the analysis of power through the empirical exploration of the interaction between individuals and social institutions.

This view of power has come under concerted criticism in recent years in the work of Foucault who opposed the idea of understanding power as the imposition of the sovereign power of centralised institutions of the state on oppressed individuals. Foucault agrees with Weber and the Frankfurt school that power in modern societies takes the form of domination, but he disagrees with their analysis that modern institutions took the position of the sovereign and individuals have the position of subjects of power. The cohesion of modern society does not result from agreement and legitimation of institutional power by citizens as autonomous individuals but results from discursive or soft power that operates through language (discourse) and the internalisation of normative social practices supported institutionally by training, surveillance and discipline (Joseph, 2003).

Foucault begins his analysis of the characteristic form of domination in modern society and its link to subjectivity in his studies of the shift in the way that modern society treated madness when compared to the medieval worldview. The mad were separated off from society, placed in a new institutional context (the asylum) and subjected to a new form of authority in the shape of the directors and doctors in the asylum who developed new forms of administrative and medical expertise. All of these changes constituted a discursive shift in the articulation of madness from something that was part of society, the locus of freedom and imagination, and instead separated it off from society, confined it and subjected it to reason in the form of forensic analysis and an ethic of self-awareness and self-control (Foucault, 1965). Foucault shifts the relationship between subjectivity and power, instead of understanding individuals as the agents and objects of power he reconfigures them as the effects of power. According to Joseph,

> It is not the individual that gives discourse meaning but the discursive formation that provides an array of subject positions that individuals occupy. Foucault leaves very little room, therefore, for

agency. So little room, in fact, that it is impossible to speak of social consent or consensus (Joseph, 2003, p. 169).

Over time, Foucault shifted away from the structuralist origins of his emphasis on discourse and opened up the analysis of disciplinary power in *Discipline and Punish* (Foucault, 1979). Foucault explains the shift to the modern period partly as the shift from punishment to discipline marked by different kinds of actions on the body of the miscreant or deviant. Punishment, in the name of the sovereign, is visited upon the body of the criminal in a spectacular, public 'theatre of pain', showing the absolute power of the sovereign (Joseph, 2003, p. 171). In contrast, Foucault argues that the modern penal system represents an attempt to reform the ethical subject through the application of surveillance, constraint and the instigation of a regime of obligation and prohibition.

The lesson that Foucault draws from this shift from punishment to discipline is critical of liberal humanism because he regards it as articulating not a shift to a shared set of liberal and humanistic values enshrined in social institutions but an expression of the needs of liberal capitalist society to become more rational through efficiency, control and standardisation. Foucault illustrated the link between liberal governance and disciplinary power through an interpretation of Bentham's prison design the 'panoptican' in which unseen guards could observe any prisoner so that the fear of observation (the internalisation of the gaze of the observer) leads the prisoner to control his or her own behaviour. For Foucault, the mental hospital and the prison were microcosms of broader processes of social cohesion in which a pure form of the interplay between discourses, institutions and practices aimed at disciplining subjects was dispersed through a range of social institutions targeted at the training of individuals in schools, the workplace and the other institutions of modern society. The similarities with Weber's accounts of discipline and rationalisation are clear, but the difference is that Foucault sees these as emerging from the combination of a discourse of exclusion and institutions organised around technologies of social control rather than through the adoption of shared values amongst bureaucrats and citizens (Dean, 1999).

Foucault developed these ideas further in his final writings on governmentality and the self. Foucault complements the idea that power is in the possession of some agents and applied to others (the capacity concept of power) with the idea that individuals are constituted as the effects of power

(Joseph, 2003, p. 179). Foucault questioned the idea that power is visited on individuals as the victims and percolated down social hierarchies. Instead, he argues that power 'is not reducible to an institution or structure, but resides in a network of strategic relations' (Joseph, 2003, p. 180). Modern forms of governing work strategically with dispersed powers using a range of techniques that normalise, regulate and control. In this practical rationality, modern forms of power are not dependent on either consent or legitimation, working through the social body rather than over it (Joseph, 2003, p. 181). Foucault provides us with a critique that brings Milgram's assumptions about power into focus. Milgram regarded power as a capacity of the authority, he embedded power in a hierarchical notion of the state and he saw the role of his participants as offering legitimacy to the power of the authority. Milgram underestimated the strategic responses of his participants to power, he did not recognise that their responses reflected a view of plural and diverse sources of power and he did not analyse the ways in which the experimental context brought the subjects of power into being.

However, although Milgram's conception of power falls neatly under the terms of Foucault's critique, we should pause to reflect on the positive qualities of Milgram's commitments. Various responses to Foucault's critique of humanism and critical theory are relevant to evaluating the contemporary relevance of Milgram's work. Milgram expresses the tradition of critique of modern society in the name of humanity and liberal democratic principles. He also asserts a view of the individual as engaged and committed to moral and political issues in contrast to the increasing individualism of modern societies. Milgram offers us a response to alienation and advocates that authority should govern and constrain itself. He also supports the pragmatist tradition advocating public intellectuals and pluralist conceptions of power and authority. All of these ideas put the individual at the centre of a range of practices that potentially liberate individuals and society from oppression and domination and from alienation and scepticism.

## Contemporary individualism: Milgram, Reality TV and virtue ethics

Milgram's approach to experimentation is intriguing because it combined elements of experimental control with observation and a focus on the experience of the participants. I have suggested, following Gitlin that Milgram's experiments as well as being impure science were part of a broader cultural reflection on the social and political settlements of post-war USA. Gitlin makes the point that culture can offer alternative perspectives in times when there is a lack of diversity in the political sphere. What was significant about Milgram and other social psychologists such as Zimbardo was that they managed to introduce the idea of the experiment as a means of exploring important social, political and moral issues focused on the unfolding of human experience in a controlled setting. The realism of these experiments has more in common with the realism of the novel than the realist assumptions of empiricist science. They embody the idea that it is possible to explore the subtle unfolding of personal events with social significance in the artificial setting of the novel (and the experiment) in a way that allows reflection on social and political issues.

Milgram's experiments have this literary and dramatic quality, and a remarkable development in popular culture takes up these themes of observing social interaction amongst a group of individuals in a controlled setting as a means of reflecting on reality: Reality TV. Reality TV has rapidly become a mainstay of television schedules across the world. Recent media analyses attempt to explain the popular appeal of Reality TV and its cultural meaning (Andrejevic, 2004; Hill, 2005; Holmes and Jermyn, 2004; Murray and Ouellette, 2004; Roscoe, 2001). One of the features of the Reality TV genre is the increasing visibility of ordinary people on television. The feelings, discussions and actions of the participants make up the content of reality shows which, like social psychology experiments, place a group of people in a contrived and loosely controlled social situation and observe their behaviour and the interactions between the participants as the show unfolds using a battery of cameras and microphones.

Although there are many different sub genres of Reality TV, a good example to illustrate the resonances between Reality TV and social psychology experiments on social influence is the reality game show exemplified by *Big Brother*. The program is located in a purpose built 'house' designed to accommodate a group of participants for the duration of the show. The participants are chosen by the production team (sometimes with the assistance of a psychologist) to reflect a diversity of personalities (e.g. extrovert and introvert), sexual identities, social backgrounds and beliefs. The first program presents background interviews with the participants. Individuals are then introduced, one by one, into the *Big Brother* house to meet their housemates. The show then runs for a period of weeks, during which time the programme directors ask participants to perform a number of game show like tasks, as well as just 'living' together in the house. A number of cameras and microphones, which cover almost every angle and space in the *Big Brother* house, record much of what occurs within its walls. The program broadcasts live and continuously on one channel and edited highlights are transmitted each evening. In addition, commentaries on the main points of interest are selected by the producers for the audience and available as a webcast. Finally, a weekly studio show presents fans and celebrities' reactions and opinions and includes the results of the vote to exclude one resident of the house a week until a winner emerges.

The audience is engaged rather than passive; in voting for evictions from the show, they are involved in the program, which gives them a sense that they can shape the events that occur within it. Annette Hill (2005) argues that watching Reality TV is not simply a passive 'space-filling' activity; audiences are critically aware of the production techniques and limitations of the format. Her close reading of audience reactions to Reality TV shows how viewers appreciate the way that such programs raise and tackle every-day dilemmas. Despite this, they understand that the programs are an artificial or constructed *mis-en-scene*, which exerts a strong influence on participants conduct. Inevitably, this means that audiences are sceptical about naïve claims to represent the real; they can see that many televised moments are inauthentic and staged. Hill's audiences, however, still claim to gain insights from such programs about styles of interaction, the psychology of relationships and the way that the situations that develop on Reality TV programs 'reveal' the character of participants.

McCarthy (2004) traces the origins of Reality TV to innovative forms of documentary, such as those developed by Alan Funt in the early 1950s. In a documentary for the *Omnibus* series, Funt pioneered the use of 'talking heads' and an observational style giving personal, first-hand accounts of working-class life in New York; this contrasted with the aesthetic of expert commentary over silent camera footage that was typical of documentary at the time. McCarthy likens Funt's innovative style to a hidden camera, which provides a naturalistic 'ethnographic' view of social life without a narrative voice-over. She suggests that Funt was influenced by, or at least that his work resonated with, the mass observation studies in the social sciences in which qualitative methods, such as depth interviewing and oral history taking, were used to document the lived experience of ordinary people. McCarthy (2004) reflects on the idea that popular culture is an expression of a radical liberal agenda and that a similar agenda preoccupied Stanley Milgram in his studies of obedience to authority. She argues that Milgram's studies of obedience to authority and Funt's documentaries both challenged traditional notions of authority and governance and were aligned to projects of reform and advocacy in civic life. Both Milgram and Funt were motivated, in their very different ways, by the desire to enhance democratic participation against the background of widespread political conformity.

In addition to the similarities in purpose between early documentary and role-play experiments in social psychology, there are similarities between Milgram's studies and *Big Brother*. The participants in both *Big Brother* and the social influence experiments are not actors, they perform unscripted actions in the sense that the participants are not instructed directly what to say and do. However, on a more subtle analysis of scripting, there are a variety of contextual influences on participants' behaviour in both cases. In both *Big Brother* and social influence experiments, the interaction between participants unfolds over time in a manufactured context with a structured cast of characters who perform specific tasks. Actors are often used as 'plants' in Reality TV to influence the action in the show just as Milgram used actors to play the roles of the experimenter and the learner. Researchers put a lot of work into creating the setting for role-play experiments: props and context provide a framework within which to observe the conduct of participants. The same is true of *Big Brother* where much thought has gone into the design and construction of a living space saturated with surveillance. In Milgram's experiments, there was no pretence that the setting did not influence the behaviour of the participants; it was intended to by placing them under certain obligations and social pressures. What is of interest, both in the social psychology experiment and the Reality TV show, is how individuals manage these pressures and how they affect their behaviour. The combination of setting and manipulation (or simulation of pressure), and the participants' reaction to events as they unfold, is what makes both Reality TV and Milgram's experiments so compelling.

These features of Reality TV resonate with role-play experiments, inviting the audience to take a position of the social psychologist by observing and interpreting the unfolding of social relationships and interaction. As with the social psychology role-play experiments, the audience of Reality

TV faces a range of dilemmas: is the observed behaviour authentic? Does the conduct of participants reflect the situation or their character? The implied audience, in the subject position of observers and interpreters of social behaviour in a controlled context, face similar interpretive, methodological and epistemological questions to the social psychologist observing and interpreting role-play experiments.

## Moral theory, virtue ethics and Reality TV

A conspicuous feature of the way that Milgram, Fromm and Riesman talk about individuals is in terms of 'character', which has fallen out of use in psychology in favour of 'temperament' and 'personality'. However, one advantage of focusing on character is that it introduces a moral dimension into social scientific reflection on individuality. The idea of good character has its origins in the moral philosophy of Plato and Aristotle, although modern moral theories shifted to a focus on moral principles and consequences. However, recently moral philosophy has re-examined questions of moral character in virtue ethics (Statman, 1997).

MacIntyre's (1981) book *After Virtue* offers an influential account of virtue ethics. MacIntyre argues that moral debates in modern societies are characterised by people adopting strong positions grounded in their personal beliefs (for example, their religious beliefs) and that this results in there being a radical incommensurability between different stances rather than arguments about principle. One consequence is that radically opposed positions on key moral debates are not resolvable through discussion and debate because they are so firmly entrenched in strongly held beliefs. Moral arguments are constrained by such beliefs. McIntyre suggests that different positions on the public debate on abortion are based on fundamental assumptions about the nature and rights of human life. Consequently, no amount of ethical debate can resolve the difference between a religious conviction that abortion is wrong and a secular position that considers medical and psychological arguments in favour of abortion rights. Consequently, there is nothing to be done except to state one's position as strongly as possible, and this reflects the nature of contemporary moral judgement and debate.

An alternative approach is to treat morality as judgements about individuals. What is good in any situation is best determined by asking what a good person would do in such circumstances. This introduces a common sense approach to moral reasoning and ethical choices. Aristotle had formalised the qualities of a good person in his theory of virtuous character. His analyses of virtue suggested the general principle that moderate character was the key to goodness. For example, courage is a virtuous character trait that falls in the middle of a dimension running from reckless bravery to cowardice both of which are vices. In this way, Aristotle sought to articulate universal features of moral character but MacIntyre reviews the historically changing list of virtues in ethical theory over the centuries and concludes that the definition of what counts as virtuous character is historically and culturally variable. For example, courage might be less relevant today whereas self-consciousness is more salient in contemporary society than in Aristotle's day. MacIntyre shifts attention away from the specific list of virtuous character traits and instead he argues that the interaction between social context and character determines what is good or bad.

MacIntyre argues that for a social context to provide the opportunity for the expression of moral character, it has to be a '... coherent and complex form of socially established co-operative human activity' (Mullhall and Swift, 1992, p. 175). The development of the skills and abilities relevant to a social practice is revealed by the process of participants getting to know each other, to intrigue, play and dispute with each other. In this sense, Milgram's experiment is a social practice that is rules based and ordered but open to change through the actions of the participants. Although they only lasted a short time, Milgram's obedience experiments constituted a social practice in a highly concentrated form, dramatically reconstructing the idea that modern life is characterised by a series of 'tests of character' in a bounded social context amongst a group of characters. The 'value' of being in such a group is as an emotional and strategic alliance in the context of the unfolding practice of the 'game' of living in the *Big Brother* house and this also explains the attempts by participants in the Milgram experiment to make sense, do the right thing and influence the course of the study. This reflects the notion of the 'language game,' where meaning is relative to a social context combining practice and convention. The isolation of the participants in *Big Brother* and the Milgram experiments constructs as an artificial anthropological community with no direct access to the outside world so that all the dynamics are contained within the unfolding of the reality show or the social psychology experiment.

The concept of the narrative unity of the self is also important to the ethics of the Milgram experiments. As I have emphasised throughout this book, the participants did not just appear from nowhere; they came with a background history, troubles and preferences. In the moral experiment of Milgram's obedience studies as in Reality TV, the participant makes the transition between the 'self' who enters the experience and the emerging 'self' that develops through interacting with other participants, as they establish alliances, rules and conventions. Much of the unstructured talking that goes on in Reality TV (often in the interstices of the game-show elements) consists of personal reflections that link the happenings in the show with the longer-term life-projects of the participants. In these moments, there is often a discussion of life before joining the show and reflections on the 'psychology' of fellow participants. We have seen also how the participants in the Milgram experiment attempt to shift the frame of reference to their lives 'outside' the experiment. The issue of self-knowledge is critical here; audiences and readers judge the participants in both Reality TV and in Milgram's experiments according to their ability to reflect honestly and with integrity and their capacity to be true to themselves while still following the rules of the social situation.

Milgram's experiments put participants in a situation that mirrored the ethical structure of modern life. They are challenged to see whether they could sustain their sense of self under pressure and deal with the responsibilities of choice in a dynamic and unfolding social context. In addition, the experiments put us, as readers, in a dual position as social scientists and moralists. We are invited, on the one hand, to observe and interpret in order to make sense of the actions and statements of the participants. Simultaneously, we are invited to judge their actions, to decide if they acted well, whether or not their actions were justifiable and to ask ourselves what we would have done in their place. The example of Reality TV demonstrates the cultural dispersal of the sensibility of Milgram the social scientist and social thinker; we are all social psychologists now.

## Conclusions

We can now see why Milgram's experiments still fascinate us. These brilliantly conceived and executed experiments raise immediate questions about moral autonomy and authority. However, they do more than that. They provide a vehicle for reflecting on the nature of individuality in modern society, demonstrate the subtle and dynamic interplay between individual and loosely bounded social practices. The experiments were the forerunner of emerging relations of power and the increasing salience of the forensic examination of character and the centrality of the individual to social life and moral judgement.

# 8 Afterword

Thomas Blass, in his excellent biography of Milgram discusses the paradoxes of Milgram's character. Milgram could be rude and ill tempered to colleagues and students but was equally capable of commitment and generosity. He could appear arrogant but also suffered periods of self-criticism and doubt that affected his work. Milgram was a larger than life character, a great talker with tremendous energy and enthusiasm which was infectious. This is evident from the way that he worked with colleagues and students on research projects where ideas were clearly picked up and pursued with determination and often a great mixture of serious mindedness and fun. All of these qualities were in evidence early on in Milgram's career when he created the experiments on obedience to authority. He had immediate success both within psychology and with the public and became what we would now call a minor celebrity. As we have seen, Milgram, through a creative fusion of ideas drawn from a variety of sources managed to distil a range of themes and questions that went to the heart of the problems facing people living in liberal democracy in a psychology experiment. Above all else, the experiment is a wonderful moment of theatre, a performance that touches concerns that are both fascinating and disconcerting. This is why his experiments have stood the test of time, not because they pin down and answer specific scientific questions but because, for a moment, science became a context for the expression of public anxiety and interest. Science had become part of the public conversation and reflection.

I have suggested that Milgram's celebrity status was in tension with the development of his ideas and his career as an academic psychologist. One incident, recounted with sympathy and care in Blass's biography, seems to me to capture this well. Blass recounts a meeting in New York in 1969 that Milgram attended at the invitation of Joseph Klapper, the director of the CBS office of social research (Blass, 2004, p. 192). Media corporations conduct a lot of research, some of it market research and ratings analysis and some social research into more fundamental issues in the relationship between media and society. Klapper solicited interest from academics into the important question of the impact of TV violence on the viewer. Milgram's studies touched on issues of aggression but it was not his focus and he had little experience of research into media effects, which was a burgeoning field, particularly in the USA. Yet Milgram was invited to the meeting and subsequently responded to the invitation to apply for funding from CBS to conduct an experimental study into media violence. He was successful in his application and received a large grant for its day of $260,000 to conduct his proposed research. As we saw in Chapter 6, Milgram attempted to make an intervention in the debate about media effects by arguing from first principles about the value of experimental research on a large scale. Milgram was clearly very persuasive, because not only did he get the grant from CBS but he also secured their agreement to film an alternative version of one of their most successful prime time drama series *Medical Center*.

Milgram found the experience enlivening including travelling to Hollywood to watch the show to be used in his experiment being filmed. This was Milgram at his best and most compelling; the visionary social scientist, intellectual, highly articulate, gregarious and with his energies and intensity fully applied to a serious social problem. I am sure he would have convinced everyone involved that great things would be achieved. As we saw, however, Milgram's confidence was misplaced. The design of his study had major methodological shortcomings, the results were ambiguous at best and the book that he produced to report the study is terrible.

Milgram, characteristically, took something from this experience. Blass reports that Milgram was fascinated by the whole process of film production and by chance, shortly afterwards was approached by Harry From, a filmmaker, who registered to do a PhD with Milgram and to work on a film based on Milgram's work on living in the city. They produced a low budget documentary film in 1972, which won a silver medal at the International Film and Television Festival in New York (Blass, 2004, p. 198). Milgram had discovered a new passion in filmmaking. This period during which he was also working on the manuscript for *Obedience to Authority* illustrates the intensity of Milgram's personal and professional life at the height of his fame. Milgram was always looking for the next idea that would attract his attention and when he found it, he would pour his energies into it, and then move on. It was clearly not his inclination to work steadily and incrementally to develop a traditional academic research career and develop his thinking and writing – he was a brilliant flame that touched on issues and then moved on.

Many people have been inspired by the audacity of Milgram's empirical work and the way that an experiment addresses important moral, political and social issues. Equally, many have been critical of Milgram on ethical, theoretical and methodological grounds. His research into obedience, the small world problem and the lost letter technique have all been highly influential and guarantee his place in the history of social psychology but his theory and his commitments to a sociological social psychology which addresses real world problems have not been so influential.

Milgram distils in a brilliant but flawed experimental design insights from sociology, politics and psychology. His experiments have meaning and importance because they link academic questions to important social issues. Milgram poses these questions in a particular form, which on the surface is a scientific experiment but in the background addresses questions that are philosophical and sociological as much as they are psychological. However, the weight of the social, political and moral questions and the relationship between theory, and social questions overburden the experiments themselves. This illustrates both the strength and the weaknesses of social psychological research. The openness of Milgram's work is a strong point because it produces research that opens up critical questions about the relationship between people and society. However, it is a weakness in that it leaves many questions unanswered at both the social and the psychological levels about the nature of society and subjectivity. Milgram himself was perhaps arrogant in believing that empirical research in social psychology could resolve the key questions of social and political theory and give us profound insights into the human condition. Perhaps it is best to think of his experiments not as resolving such questions but as articulating them, demonstrating them in a way that reminds us of the dangers of power and the vulnerability of individuals, opening up questions of power, political subjectivity and moral responsibility in modern society.

Although Milgram was committed to the idea that social psychology should address the key social issues of the day and connect with intellectual themes in philosophy and social theory it is not always clear what he sees as the purpose of this engagement. Milgram often uses the Holocaust as the background to his work and yet at other moments appears to be saying that the focus of his work is the social and political conditions of the USA in the late 1950s and early 1960s. I believe that his main concerns were with political apathy, the alienation of life in the city and the barriers to human potential in modern society. However, the way that the liberal democracy of the Weimar republic was politically vulnerable and gave way to fascism left a strong impression on Milgram. This is why Milgram sought to demonstrate the vulnerability of individuals to social influence and he complemented this with his view that liberal democracy was fragile and open to control by powerful groups or to the demands of popular democracy. As a public intellectual Milgram thought that his responsibility was to bring these issues to public attention so that politicians would be on guard against excesses of power and limit their activities and that individuals would become conscious of their own vulnerability so that they would be watchful of attempts to influence them. Milgram was a rationalist, a liberal and a humanist but also an elitist. This became clear as Milgram became increasingly uncomfortable with the deployment of social conflict in the protest movements of the late 1960s and early 1970s as a means of promoting social change. Milgram favoured an ordered and orderly society.

Milgram was concerned with theoretical questions of social and political theory and questions of moral philosophy; he was primarily concerned with the human condition. His starting point was that humans were social animals displaced from their natural habitat to live in the cities of the modern world. The human condition in modernity involved the dangers of isolation, fragmentation of communities and the vulnerability of individuals. However, although he recognised these dangers, Milgram had confidence in the capability of individuals to find ways of connecting with others and coping with modern society. In his later empirical work, Milgram demonstrated that human beings found solutions to the complexity and alienation of modern society through their network of social contacts, by sharing meaningful representations of the cities they inhabit, by forming coherent and manageable groups. However, there was one potential danger that individuals would have little defence against that was a hang over from our evolutionary heritage and resulted in our disposition to obey authority. He believed that social hierarchies protect individuals but that our trusting nature leaves us open to manipulation and social control. Milgram's experiments mirrored the potential for social control in liberal democracies and demonstrated the vulnerability of individuals to malevolent authority in totalitarian regimes.

Although Milgram's interests and concerns were wide ranging, he remained a strong advocate of social psychology and through his research and writing developed a particular view of the nature and role of social psychology. He connected social psychology to the other social sciences, especially in establishing research questions but he retained a strong sense of the uniqueness of social psychology in adopting methods of observation and experimentation focused on the experience of individuals living in a social world. He gave particular emphasis to the idea that social, political and moral theories made strong assumptions about the experiences and conduct of individuals but that only social psychology could test these. His commitment to the individual was both personal and political. He wanted to protect and enable the capacity of individuals because he placed a high value on autonomy and freedom and he saw in the undermining of individuals the routes of totalitarianism.

Milgram was at his best when designing and conducting empirical social psychology studies aimed at social questions. He was innovative and creative in his use of methods. Milgram can be criticised for not working out the relationship between his empirical material and social questions and for a lack of depth in interpretation. However, to some degree these criticisms miss the point because in Milgram's view empirical research was as much oriented to opening up and posing questions, as it was to addressing specific research hypotheses. Milgram's empirical research was expansive in scope and experimental in the broader sense of trying out methods and addressing social questions through empirical examples. This partly explains the continuing relevance of Milgram's work because he was addressing questions that retain their significance related to the nature of liberal democracy and power and the experience of being an individual in modern society.

Milgram was a heroic, renaissance figure, a filmmaker, researcher, teacher and public intellectual. He put social psychology into the public eye and confronted questions of enormous moral and political significance. He was a charismatic figure with an idiosyncratic approach to social psychology, a creative researcher, brilliant speaker and a committed liberal humanist who was concerned about the vulnerability of democracy. However, he was also a paradoxical figure: liberal but not radical; optimistic about humanity but pessimistic about power; a scientist but also a filmmaker; enormously successful but prone to self doubt; a leader in his field but thoroughly controversial. We will be lucky to see his like again in social psychology.

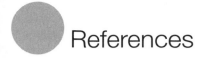

# References

T. W. Adorno, E. Frenkel-Brunswik, D. J. Levinson, and R. N. Sanford, *The Authoritarian Personality*, (New York: Harper and Row, 1950).

M. Andrejevic, *Reality TV: The work of being watched*, (Oxford: Rowman & Littlefield, 2004).

H. Arendt, *Eichman in Jerusalem: A report on the banality of evil*, (New York: Viking Press, 1963).

S. Asch, *Social Psychology*, (Englewood Cliffs, NJ: Prentice Hall, 1952).

Z. Bauman, *Modernity and the Holocaust*, (Cambridge: Polity, 1989).

D. Baumrind, 'Some thoughts on ethics of research: After reading Milgram's "behavioral study of obedience"', *American Psychologist* 19 (1964), 421–423.

I. Berlin, 1969, 'Two concepts of liberty', in I. Berlin, *Four Essays on Liberty*, (Oxford: Oxford University Press, 1969).

L. Bortolotti and M. Mameli, 'Deception in psychology: moral costs and benefits of unsought for knowledge', *Accountability in Research*, 13 (2006) 259–275.

T. Blass, *The Man Who Shocked the World: The life and legacy of Stanley Milgram*, (Cambridge, Mass.: Basic Books, 2004).

T. Blass, *Obedience to Authority: Current perspectives on the Milgram paradigm*, (Mahwah, NJ.: Lawrence Erlbaum Associates, 2000).

R. Brown, *Social Psychology: The second edition*, (New York: The Free Press, 1986).

I. Carter, 'Positive and negative liberty', *Stanford Encyclopaedia of Philosophy*, Oct 8, 2007, URL = http://plato.stanford.edu/entries/liberty-positive-negative/.

M. de Certeau, *The Practice of Everyday Life,* trans. Steven Rendall, (Berkeley: University of California Press, 1984).

D. Cesarani, *Eichmann: His life and crimes*, (London: Heinemann, 2004).

R. Dahl, *A Preface to Democratic Theory*, (Chicago: University of Chicago Press, 1956).

M. Dean, *Governmentality: Power and rule in modern society*, (London: Sage, 1999).

J. M. Doris, *Lack of Character: Personality and moral behaviour*, (New York: Cambridge University Press, 2002).

R. J. Evans, *The Third Reich in Power*, (London: Penguin Books, 2006).

S. Feshback and R. D. Singer, *Television and Aggression*, (San Francisco: Jossey-Bass, 1971).

L. Festinger and J. M. Carlsmith, 'Cognitive consequences of forced compliance', *Journal of Abnormal and Social Psychology*, 58 (1959) 203–210.

M. Foucault, *Madness and Civilization. A History of Insanity in the Age of Reason*, (New York: Pantheon Books, 1965).

M. Foucault, *Discipline and Punish: The birth of the prison*, (London: Penguin, 1979).

E. Fromm, *Escape From Freedom*, (New York: Holt, Rinehart and Winston, 1941).

J. L. Gaddis, *The Cold War*, (New York: Penguin Books, 2005).

W. A. Gamson, B. Fireman and S. Rytina, *Encounters with Unjust Authority*, (Homewood, Ill.: Dorsey Press, 1982).

G. Gerbner, 'Communication and social environment', *Scientific American*, 227 (1972) 153–160.

A. Giddens, *Modernity and Self Identity*, (Cambridge: Polity Press, 1991).

T. Gitlin, *The Sixties: Years of hope, days of rage*, (New York: Bantam Books, 1987).

E. Goffman, *The Presentation of Self in Everyday Life*, (New York: Doubleday Anchor Books, 1959).

G. Harman, 'Moral philosophy meets social psychology: virtue ethics and the fundamental attribution error', *Proceedings of the Aristotelian Society*, 99 (1999) 315–331.

R. Harré, *Social Being*, (Oxford: Blackwell, 1979).

S. A. Haslam and S. Reicher, 'Beyond the banality of evil: three dynamics of an interactionist social psychology of tyranny', *Personality and Social Psychology Bulletin*, 33 (2007) 615–622.

D. Held, *Introduction to Critical Theory: Horkheimer to Habermas*, (Cambridge: Polity Press, 1980).

D. Held, *Models of Democracy*, 3rd Edn. (Cambridge: Polity Press, 2007).

A. Hill, *Reality TV: Audiences and popular factual television*, (London: Routledge, 2005).

H. Himmelweit, A. N. Oppenheim and P. Vance, *Television and the Child: An empirical study of the effect of television on the young*, (Oxford: Oxford University Press, 1958).

S. Holmes and D. Jermyn, *Understanding Reality Television*, (London: Routledge, 2004).

A. Jamison and R. Eyerman, *Seeds of the Sixties*, (Berkeley: University of California, 1994).

I. L. Janis and B. T. King, 'The influence of role-playing on opinion change', *Journal of Abnormal and Social Psychology*, 49 (1954) 211–218.

J. Joseph, *Social Theory: Conflict, cohesion and consent*, (Edinburgh: Edinburgh University Press, 2003).

H. C. Kelman, 'Human Use Of Human Subjects: The problem of deception in social psychological experiments', *Psychological Bulletin*, 67 (1967) 1–11.

N. Klein, *The Shock Doctrine*, (London: Penguin Books, 2007).

G. M. Kren and L. Rappoport, *The Holocaust and the Crisis of Human Behavior*, revised edition, (New York: Holmes & Meier, 1994).

R. T. LaPiere, (1934) 'Attitudes vs actions', *Social Forces*, 13, 230–237.

B. Latané, 'The psychology of social impact', *American Psychologist*, 36 (1981) 343–356.

G. Le Bon, *The Crowd*, (London: Transaction Publishers, 1999).

K. Lewin, *Field Theory in Social Science*, (New York: Harper, 1951).

S. M. Lipset and S. S. Wolin, *The Berkeley Student Revolt: Facts and interpretations*, (New York: Doubleday Anchor, 1965).

A. MacIntyre, *After Virtue: A study in moral theory*, (London: Duckworth, 1981).

A. McCarthy, 'Stanley Milgram, Alan Funt, and me', in S. Murray and L. Ouellette, *Reality TV: Remaking television culture*, (New York: New York University Press, 2004).

A. McCoy, *A Question of Torture: CIA interrogation, from the Cold War to the War on Terror*, (New York: Metropolitan Books, 2006).

C. Marsh, A science museum exhibit on Milgram's obedience research: history, description and visitors' reactions. In Thomas Blass (ed.) (op cit., 2000).

G. H. Mead, *Mind, Self and Society*, ed. C.W. Morris (Chicago: University of Chicago, 1934).

S. Milgram, 'Behavioral study of obedience', *Journal of Abnormal and Social Psychology*, 67 (1963) 371–378.

S. Milgram, 'Some conditions of obedience and disobedience to authority', *Human Relations*, 18 (1965) 57–76.

S. Milgram, *Obedience to Authority: An experimental view*, (New York: Harper and Row, 1974).

S. Milgram, *The Individual in a Social World*, (Reading, Mass.: Addison-Wesley Publishing Company, 1977).

S. Milgram, *Television and Antisocial Behavior*, (New York: Academic Press, 1973).

A. G. Miller, *The Obedience Experiments: A case study of controversy in social science*, (New York: Praeger, 1986).

D. Mixon, 'Instead of deception', *Journal for the Theory of Social Behaviour*, 2 (1972) 145–174.

D. Mixon, 'Studying feignable behaviour', *Representative Research in Social Psychology*, 7 (1976) 89–104.

D. Mixon, 'Why pretend to deceive?', *Personality and Social Psychology Bulletin*, 3 (1977) 647–653.

S. Mulhall and A. Swift, *Liberals and Communitarians*, (Oxford: Blackwell, 1992).

S. Murray and L. Ouellette, *Reality TV: Remaking television culture*, (New York: New York University Press, 2004).

E. Noelle-Neumann, *The Spiral of Silence: Public opinion: Our social skin*, (Chicago: University of Chicago Press, 1993).

M. T. Orne, 'On the social psychology of the psychological experiment: with particular reference to demand characteristics and their implications', *American Psychologist*, 17 (1962) 776–783.

M. T. Orne and C. H. Holland, 'On the ecological validity of laboratory deception', *International Journal of Psychiatry*, 6 (1968) 282–293.

K. Pandora, *Rebels Within the Ranks: Psychologists' critique of scientific authority and democratic realities in new deal America*, (Cambridge: Cambridge University Press, 1997).

T. Parsons, *The Structure of Social Action*, (New York: McGraw Hill, 1937).

T. Parsons, *The Social System*, (Chicago: Free Press, 1951).

R. D. Putnam, *Bowling Alone: The collapse and revival of American community*, (New York: Simon and Schuster, 2000).

S. D. Reicher and S. A. Haslam, 'Rethinking the psychology of tyranny: the BBC prison study', *British Journal of Social Psychology*, 45 (2006) 1–40.

S. Riesman, N. Glazer and R. Denney, *The Lonely Crowd: A study of the changing American character*, (New York: Doubleday Anchor, 1950).

J. Roscoe, 'Big brother Australia: performing the "real" twenty-four-seven', *International Journal of Cultural Studies*, 4 (2001) 473–488.

J. Schumpeter, *Capitalism, Socialism and Democracy*, (London: Allen and Irwin, 1976).

N. Smelser, *Theory of Collective Behavior*, (New York: Free Press, 1963).

D. Statman, (ed.), *Virtue Ethics: A critical reader*, (Edinburgh: Edinburgh University Press, 1997).

R. Stevens, *Freud: Examining the essence of his contribution*, (Basingstoke: Palgrave Macmillan, 2008).

A. Thompson, *Erich Fromm: Enquirer into the human condition*, (Basingstoke: Palgrave Macmillan, 2009).

M. Weber, *Economy and Society: An outline of interpretive sociology*, (New York: Bedminster Press, 1968).

H. Zinn, *A People's History of the United States*, (New York: Harper & Row, 1980).

# Index